Warren Macdonald grew up in Melbourne's west, a true product of the 'burbs. His forays into the bush and extensive travel, however, changed his perspective on life.

His love of bushwalking and the natural world led him to become a committed environmentalist. He spent 12 months of his life dedicated to the cause of keeping Tasmania's Tarkine region free from an intrusive road, and remains deeply saddened that he and his friends were unable to stop the destruction they witnessed.

Deeply in tune with the bush, he received his calling with the opportunity for formal qualifications in the field of outdoor adventure guiding. He recognised that, through giving people a wilderness experience, he may foster a respect for the Earth in someone otherwise indifferent to events outside their own environment. This remains one of his goals.

He currently lives in Melbourne, working as a climbing instructor in an indoor climbing gym. Still climbing mountains, most recently Tasmania's Federation Peak in an epic four-week adventure, he now uses a specially developed pair of prosthetic 'legs' rather than the seat of his pants, though he prefers the wheelchair for everyday life around town, as the 'legs' slow him down too much.

He yearns for the day when he finally realises he can't possibly do 'everything' he wants to do, and begins to appreciate again the simple pleasure of sleeping under a tree for hours on end!

For more information, check out Warren's website at www.partanimal.com

ONE STEP BEYOND

WARREN MACDONALD

Hardie Grant Books

First published in 1999
by Hardie Grant Publishing
Level 3, 44 Caroline Street
South Yarra Victoria 3141
New edition published in 1999
Reprinted in 1999 and 2000

National Library of Australia Cataloguing-in-Publication data:
  Warren Macdonald
  One step beyond
  ISBN 1 86498 101 6

  1. Macdonald, Warren. 2. Mountaineers — Australia — Biography.
  3. Mountaineering accidents — Queensland — Hinchinbrook Island.
  4. Mountaineering injuries — Queensland — Hinchinbrook Island.
  I. Title.

  796.522092

Illustrations by Geert van Keulen
Cover and text design by Philip Campbell
Typeset by Melbourne Media Services
Produced by Griffin Press
Printed and bound in Adelaide

For Matthew, Jordan and Samantha; when they are old enough
to understand.

ACKNOWLEDGEMENTS

I would like to thank:

All at Queensland Emergency Services for their role in my rescue, in particular Dany Portefaix (crewman – my apologies for the South African reference in earlier editions), Greg Beer (winchman), Tim Kesteven (helicopter pilot) and Bill Johnstone (airport fire officer).

Dr Chip Jaffurs MD for keeping me alive untill we reached Cairns Base Hospital.

'Goody' the ferryman, for a job well done.

The staff who looked after me at the Cairns Base Hospital, including: Surgeon Bill Clark, Dr John Morgan, Dr Lara Weiland, Dr Katherine Swanson, Roger, and others whose names have escaped me. To those few who didn't look after me, well . . .

My family, especially Mum and Dad for being there for me the whole time in Cairns.

Elaine and Wal McCulloch.

Belinda Wells and Natalie Dudding for coming when I needed them most.

Paul and Karen Wilson.

Rob and Tina Baines for packing up my gear and getting it, along with my car, back to Melbourne.

North East Highlands Forest Action Group for holding the 'Wazza Bash'.

Steph for holding the raffle.

Everybody who helped with my Cradle Mountain climb, of whom there are far too many to mention.

The following businesses for their help and support:

Bogong Equipment
Mont Adventure Equipment
Sonar Wetsuits
Toshiba Australia
Intermedia Works
Qantas Airways

Everyone who helped me at the Royal Talbot Rehabilitation Centre, including Elaine Drews for my climbing shorts.

Daphne Smith for her friendship and support.

Selina Byrne and Cath Tregillis from the Commonwealth Rehabilitation Service for their encouragement and advice.

Deidre McEwan and Harm Ellens for getting me started in the world of computers.

Leanne Kennedy for putting up with me while I wrote this book.

And last, but not least:

Geert van Keulen for doing what he had to do, and for doing it well. Also for his generous contribution in the telling of his side of quite a remarkable story.

My apologies to all I have failed to mention, and there will be many. You know who you are.

CONTENTS

FOREWORD BY CHIP JAFFURS, MD

Certain things in life begin as if in a dream. The circumstances are not to be immediately believed but the reality is assertive. Our minds project a protective dreamlike caste to the situation and we can therefore function. I clearly recall this perception as I answered the Emergency Department's helicopter hotline late one afternoon. The situation brief was a disjointed list of facts, and a request for urgent assistance. Trapped under a boulder near a mountaintop, partner hiked out for help, calling from a boat, come quickly, he's been under the rock for two days.

The minutes and hours continued to slip by as we assembled a rescue team and its gear. It was almost dusk as we hovered over Hinchinbrook Island off the coast of tropical Far North Queensland.

Below in the scrub we would find a most remarkable human being. He would be reclining in a stream, a crushed and quiet body harbouring the smallest spark of life. I'm still not sure how much I helped Warren Macdonald. I remain grateful for the skill and tenacity of the Queensland Rescue crew who got us all off that pitch black mountainside, but my morphine and intravenous fluids were just a checking manoeuvre for this individual. He grabbed a hold on life as it slithered away from him, held on, and never looked back.

Later I recalled his hoarse whispers telling me that he most certainly knew that if the helicopter hadn't come for him by sundown that he would die.

Warren Macdonald would live, though in a dream that few of us can imagine. I still hear from him from time to time, as I make my way through an all too normal life. I marvel at his steady determination and optimism.

Perhaps I also wonder whether, faced with the same challenge, I could do so well.

Whangarei, New Zealand, November 1998

FOREWORD BY BRIAN HALL

An old lady sits in her sunny room at a hostel for the aged, peering out the window at the colourful spring roses that have burst into bloom. She is an important lady; she is my grandmother. Unfortunately she has Alzheimer's disease. A lifetime of memories is stored away in her head: love, death, war, all of the experiences and hardships that growing up on an island can present, all filed away and more importantly recalled in an instant.

'Did you go outside for a walk yesterday Nan?' I ask. She looks back quizzically at me, almost painfully.

'I can't remember, dear. I'm getting old. I'm eighty-six, you know!'

Should I be worried or concerned? I think not.

This is the lady who told me years ago: 'It's the challenges you over-come in life that define the person you are' — something I have applied to my personal and professional life ever since. After all, is it more important for each of us to remember what we did yesterday or to remember the people and events that have shaped our being, from seventy years ago, as my grandmother can?

We all face challenges; it is just the gravity of the solution that is different.

Warren Macdonald has faced many challenges already in his life. Some he has actively sought to experience, others he has not. He is an earthy sort of fellow, strong, lean and with a sense of purpose that you don't see in many people. You somehow sense he is going somewhere, he knows what he wants out of his endeavours, his life seems sorted and defined.

I first met Warren ('Wazza') Macdonald in an interview for an adventure tourism training course, and in our ensuing relationship I have been privileged to be enriched by his determination, strength of spirit and acceptance of the mysterious adventure called life in which we all take part.

Wazza is a friend to many. His concern for his fellow human being and for the natural world is, in a word, passionate. Needless to say, this concern was repaid after news had broken of an accident involving a bushwalker on Hinchinbrook Island. A car-sized boulder had pinned Warren in a creek bed for nearly two days. Surrounded by the constant noise of rising water, he was alone — with his pain and his thoughts.

Cairns Base Hospital is a long way from Tasmania, and I felt every mile of it as I made repeated attempts to contact Wazza, eventually speaking to him after yet another unsuccessful attempt by doctors to salvage something of his legs. He retold the story with a composed and black and white view of his experience, as only Wazza could.

'Shit, mate. You're joking. Shit,' was the only response I could muster at the time.

Weeks and months passed, rehab started and our conversations changed from reflective to futuristic. Wazza wanted to see part of the Tasmanian wilderness again. The last mountain he had climbed before the accident was on the adventure tourism course. He wanted to climb it again. It was Cradle Mountain, in the northern Tasmania highlands.

Hundreds of thousands of people go to view Cradle Mountain each year. There are carloads and busloads of them. It is one of Tasmania's most photographed and easily accessed mountains — simply because you can drive there. If you want to see the view from the top, however, you have to climb it; and it isn't an easy climb. Steep glacial carved valley walls and exposed alpine plateaus lead to the foot of the mountain. From there the scree covered flanks of the 'cradle' lead to dolerite cliffs and amphitheatres before finally the summit is seen.

No one had tried anything like this before as far as we knew. It didn't really matter if they had, because the sole drive behind it was one man's wish to stand, literally, again on top of the mountain, to prove to himself and to the community at large that we are all capable of extraordinary accomplishments. It was his baby. We were all simply privileged onlookers to what would become an inspirational and triumphant accomplishment.

Indeed, if there was ever an example of 'it's the challenges you overcome in life that define the person you are', this had to be it.

Wazza's story is simply breathtaking in its determination.

Hobart, December 1998

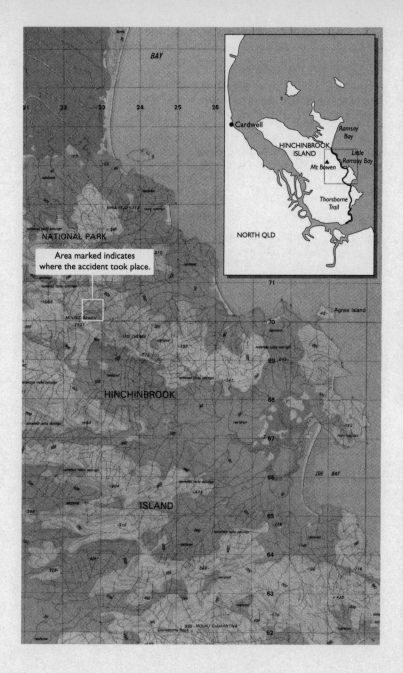

Area marked indicates
where the accident took place.

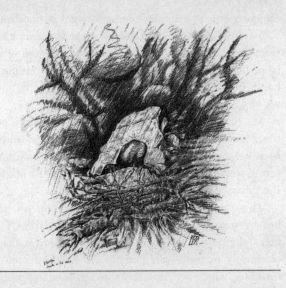

PART 1 THE ROAD LESS TRAVELLED

'God be with those who explore in the cause of under-standing; whose search takes them far from what is familiar and comfortable and leads them into danger or terrifying loneliness. Let us try to understand their sometimes strange or difficult ways; their confronting or unusual language; the uncommon life of their emotions, for they have been affected and shaped and changed by their struggle at the frontiers of a wild dark-ness, just as we may be affected, shaped and changed by the insights they bring back to us. Bless them with strength and peace. Amen.'

Michael Leunig

THE FINAL STEP

Stepping ever so carefully, edging forward in the dark, I make my way across the narrow creek bed. With no recent rain, it's almost dry, apart from the thin trickle down the centre, the sound of which is all that's to be heard — that, and the rustling of Geert settling into his sleeping bag behind me — in a night illuminated softly by the blanket of stars above.

My bare feet probing forward, I pull back from contact with cool moss, tempting me to slide across its surface, and search instead for dry rock before shifting my weight forward. A few more steps and I'm across, reaching out in the dark for the granite bank I need to climb if I'm going to get any distance from this creek.

This was turning into a bit of a mission just to go for a leak, but having had more than one dose of giardia, I wasn't about to break the golden rule and do it anywhere near the water. So many seemingly pristine watercourses are now infected with this intestinal bug, which is transmitted through human waste and usually only clears up with a course of antibiotics. You should always go at least 50 metres from any creek or stream, double that if you've got other intentions.

Once over this embankment, I should be far enough away. My groping fingers, feeling their way across the rock's surface, discover a crack, easily deep enough for me to get a good hold. I follow it along to a comfortable height and begin searching with my right hand for a second hold. *OK. So far, so good*.

Raising my left leg, I place the foot in several positions, rocking forward slightly, searching for the right balance between hands and foot. Geert is silent now, settled into his bag under the safety of my thin nylon tarp. The soft murmur of mountain juices bubbling, descending towards the sea, their journey just begun, is now the only sound in the still of night.

Confident of my hold, I push through the left leg, simultaneously pulling up with my left hand. Suddenly, there's a loud crack! In that split second, I feel my balance go as the world beneath me gives way.

Another crack (my pelvis fracturing, I was to later learn), then a crying-out, no words — just a groan, forced out as I tensed on impact, my diaphragm pushed upwards, hard. Pain comes instantly, a sharp burning pain, shooting up from my lower body. I've got no idea what's happened at first — the actual fall, even now, gone from my memory, removed perhaps to protect me. *I can't move! Something's on top of me!* Crushing me against the rocks below. *What's happening! What the fuck's going on!* I reach down frantically and feel cold, rough stone. Then, comprehension of what's happened hits me like a steam train and I push frantically with all my might — nothing moves — the pain unbearable in my legs and pelvis, searing and grinding, like nothing I have felt before, as I begin to struggle violently from side to side, trying to wriggle free.

'Fuck!' I cry out in agony. 'Grab the torch!'

Geert is quickly unzipping his sleeping bag. 'What? What's happened? Warren, are you all right?'

'Mate, quick, bring the torch!' I breathe out heavily as I struggle to push myself free.

Scrambling quickly across the slimy rocks, torch beam flashing wildly, Geert is trying to make some sense of the scene sporadically lit before him as he gets closer.

'What's happened?' he shouts nervously, moving faster now. From the pain and urgency in my voice, and the sight unfolding in the torch-light as he reaches my side, it becomes clear to him that I'm in serious trouble.

'Aaagh, mate, here!' I plead. 'Help me, push here!' He crouches quickly down beside me, trying to gain footing on the slippery rock, feet splashing in the shallow water.

'All right, here?'

'Uuugh!' I groan, chest heaving with my fast, deep breathing. 'Y-yeah, here, quick!'

'OK, push!' We both push with all our combined strength, the kind of strength that comes from within, tapped from some primitive source deep in the mind that somehow overrides all the warning signals, lets you push your body beyond its own pain barrier.

I'm pushing so hard, I feel as if I'm almost pulling myself apart, trying to leave my trapped half behind, searing pain flaring in my upper thighs. Nothing moves and I cry out in despair, 'Noooooooo!' My head and shoulders are thrown back in agony, the weight grinding down into my lap.

'Oh, faaark,' I howl. 'Go, again!' My heaving voice full of urgency and desperation.

'OK, hang on mate!' Geert frantically tries to gain some footing against the slimy rock before bracing himself to go again. 'All right, go!'

We both push again with all our might, faces grimacing in pain, muscles ready to explode. Pushing. Pushing. Pushing urgently. 'C'monnnn!' I cry out.

It doesn't move. Not an inch. Not even a millimetre.

'Aaaaaaaagh! C'monnnnn!'

We're both still pushing, with whatever's left. Pushing until there is nothing. I collapse backwards, exhausted. Geert leans forward, head down, breathing hard.

OK. Calm, calm. Got to stay calm, I keep telling myself, over and over. Leaning forward, then back, trying to reduce the pain, get some kind of release from it. None comes. I sit there, face screwed up in pain, trying to come to grips with what's happened.

'Are you OK, mate?'

'Yep. Yeah, I think I'm OK.' I take a deep breath.

Somehow, very calmly, I set about giving Geert instructions as if the foreman in charge of a building project.

'Mate, what we've got to do is' — another deep breath, grimacing in pain — 'we need to get a branch, or a small tree.' Another pause. 'Something strong, for a lever.'

'OK,' says Geert, shining the torch along the bank quickly, back and forward, left and right.

'Over there, try over there,' I say, as the beam lights up a stand of saplings, smooth-barked water gums rising above sedge grass and stunted banksias lining the bank.

Eyes closed now, breathing deeply, trying to slow it down, trying to slow my heart, which right now feels like it's trying to burst out of my chest. *C'mon, calm, calm*. I keep telling myself, over and over, *You've got to stay calm. All right!*

Geert puts a hand on my shoulder reassuringly. 'OK, mate, you're gonna be OK. I'll be as quick as I can, just hang in there, we'll get you out of here.' As he heads towards the gums, I feel the first spots of rain. I look up into a black sky, the pitter-patter of raindrops increasing steadily. *No, not now. Please, not now!*

Time passes in slow motion as I lie slumped over the slab, waiting. I can hear Geert in the trees. Wrenching and pulling, the *swoosh-swoosh* of leaves against each other as he whips a branch back and forth violently. I listen intently when he stops, picturing him moving on to another, something he has more chance of breaking. Willing him on in my mind, fighting the pain rising inside me, the fear. More swooshing, then CRACK! I pray he'll be quick. I can see the sabre of light moving wildly up on the bank, throwing thousands of shadows all around the shallow gorge. Then he's heading back, branch slung over one shoulder, torch in the other hand throwing light across a now dangerously slippery bed of stone. He slips, recovering well before continuing towards me.

Suddenly realising my total vulnerability, my absolute reliance on another human being, sends more than a cold shiver down my spine. The very thought hits me like an electric shock, my mind spinning so fast I can almost hear the whirr.

'Bloody hell, mate. Be careful. Just take your time.' I start to shake.

'OK, where do you want it?'

'Under here. See where my leg is?' My left leg lies twisted under the granite slab out of sight, but the right has only just been caught, one edge of the stone hanging over it by just ten or fifteen centimetres. This makes the leg visible from the knee down if I lean forward and over to my right, leaving a space beside it to introduce a lever. Geert slides the limb under the overhang, lifting until he finds the ceiling, his end now just under shoulder height. 'OK, are you ready?'

I've got both hands on the rock, ready to push. 'Yeah, go for it!'

Bending his knees, Geert pushes up hard, grunting with effort, his whole body straining. I push as hard as I can, trying to lift and slide myself out at once. The rock seems to shift momentarily and I push with all my might.

'Faaaaaaaark!' I cry out as my bare skin shears under the rough stone, scraping horribly as I drag myself back a few inches. I double over in agony at the shift in weight from my pelvis to my upper thighs as Geert, unable to hold it any longer, lowers his end. It feels as if it's just fallen on me all over again.

I cry out 'Again, quick!' reeling from the pain. Responding instantly, he lifts again, grunting loudly, straining with the effort. I'm pushing with everything I've got, and more, but I still can't move. *Lift! Higher! Higher!* Wriggling frantically to break free, even more determined after my taste of success.

A CRACK! signals the end of our natural crowbar, both of us still pushing, unwilling to accept our failure. Geert keeps lifting until the end is splintered like a Smith Street Mohawk.

'Faaaaaaaarkin' helllllll! Nooooooo!'

I start to feel really scared; it's raining hard now. For the first time, I start to think I might not be coming out of this. *No way! Don't even think about it!* But it's no good. I am still scared.

'We need another one.'

Deep breath.

'Something stronger, maybe a small tree.'

Another.

'You'll have to get it out of the ground somehow, mate.'

Geert's nodding, kneeling beside me, 'OK, hang in there, you're gonna be all right.' With that, he's off, back downstream a little, then up the bank into the trees. I lie back, exhausted, shaking my head in pain and disbelief. It's raining harder now. I scan the sky for some sign of a clearing but there's nothing — just black. This can't be happening, it's bullshit. Time seems to be standing still, it feels like hours before he returns. It's probably more like 20 or 30 minutes.

Carrying a whole young tree stripped of leaves, carefully making his way across the bouldered creek bed, Geert looks exhausted. The butt of the sapling is split and splintered where he's had to wrestle it from its roots, using his Swiss Army knife to cut the tough, green shards so unwilling to let go. Swiss Army knives were never designed to cut down trees. I can see now exactly which tool we need and, unfortunately, we don't have it.

Twelve months earlier, whilst living down in Tasmania, I had done a four-week introductory course in outdoor adventure tour guiding. One afternoon lecture saw our instructor, and since then a good friend of mine, Brian Hall, empty the contents of his backpack onto the table. He proceeded to describe the purpose and relevance of each item of equipment required for a typical overnight hike. Everything was pretty standard till he pulled out what looked like a very large pocket knife, except instead of a knife blade it had a 15 or 20 centimetre length of bush saw blade folded inside. His theory being that, in a situation where an injured party needs to be carried out, you're going to need to construct a stretcher. To do that requires a number of strong poles and to get strong poles requires some type of cutting. If you can manage to break them off by hand, they're not going to be able to support somebody's weight safely for any length of time, especially if the rescue is over or through rough terrain.

The fact that Geert had been able to break these branches off with his bare hands and a pocket knife meant we didn't have a hope in hell of lifting a rock later estimated to weigh a ton with one of them.

It's not long before this one, too, gives way, slowly creaking before cracking and splintering under pressure. *No-o-o-o! This can't be happening...it can't! I've got to get out!*

We both lie back, exhausted, a mixture of sweat and drizzling rain running down both our faces. Leaning forward, I slump over the slab, like I'm sitting at a desk. In absolute despair, I feel like just giving up and sobbing into the stone. But something in me won't allow it. I snap back to reality, back into focus.

'There's got to be a better way. We've got to try something else. Let's just have a rest for a minute and think about this.'

'Are you warm enough, Warren?' Geert asks as he crosses the creek to the camp. Then, before I can answer, adds, 'Where's your sleeping bag?'

'Under the tarp, in the green stuff-sack,' I reply. The mention of my sleeping bag reminds me that I should be in it now. Under the tarp. Fast asleep. Instead, I'm caught in a nightmare. A real one that I can't hope to just wake from and be OK. Watching Geert on the other side of the creek, under the tarp, I envy his freedom.

He returns with both our jackets, and my sleeping bag, which he pulls from its cover. He helps me wrap it around my waist. The rain is getting heavier and my woollen vest is now covered with tiny droplets of water that soak in when I brush them. Putting the jacket on, I realise how cold I've become and appreciate the warmth it offers. I almost left it back in Cardwell, somewhat suspect of the merit of Gore-Tex in the tropics. I decided at the last minute that it didn't take up much space, is relatively light and, who knows, it just might come in handy.

Geert puts his own jacket on, then sits down beside me and

massages my shoulders to comfort me, making me feel so glad I'm not alone. Then, with cold, wet hands, he somehow rolls himself a smoke under the shelter of his jacket hood, anxious for the nicotine's calming effect. *Maybe he's one of these blokes that could roll a cigarette under water if they had to.*

I'm amazed at how clearly my mind is operating now, deliberate and calculating, recognising the danger I'm in and the need for logical, positive action. There must be a way! I reason, and suddenly an idea springs forth.

'Rocks, we need some rocks, about this size [I shape a twenty-five to thirty centimetre square], down here, alongside my right leg.'

While Geert gathers them, throwing them just to the side of me, I begin setting them one on the other until I have a pillar reaching just below the ceiling of the mantle overhanging my right knee. Selecting a wedge-shaped stone and holding it in place with my left hand, I begin belting it with another in my right. I get the wedge held in place, but can't hit it hard enough to accomplish any more from my awkward position.

'Geert, give me a hand here. This might do it.' I lean as far as I can to my left as he takes over the assault, driving the stone in as hard as possible.

'That's it. Keep going, mate. I like it. I like what I see here.' The slab tilts slightly, easing the pressure on my right leg but transferring it instantly to my left. My whole body tenses with pain as my left leg is so badly crushed that it feels like it will actually split open.

'Mate! Stop!' I cry out, then fall back in agony. It seems like an eternity before I become accustomed to this latest version of pain — an incredible burning, as if the temperature has been turned up again.

Fear descended over me like a dark cloud, the enormity of the situation becoming clearer, my mind no longer being able to refuse to accept completely the fact that I was trapped. Trapped under a massive rock in the middle of a creek bed, in the pouring rain, eight hours' walk from the nearest track, on a remote island. *This really can't be happening, can it?*

Still struggling to accept my predicament, I realise something that makes me feel sick in the pit of my stomach, like I've just swallowed a large piece of ice. *The creek is rising.*

Whereas my arse had hardly been touching the water in the beginning, I was now sitting in the middle of a rising creek with water swirling around my mid-thigh. It had risen at least seven to ten centimetres since the rain began, and that was only a few hours ago.

No, it can't come up much further, can it? What am I going to do if it comes up higher? I'm trying really hard to ignore that line of thought. *Mate, don't even think about it.*

'We need another branch, Geert. With you levering, and me using the rocks as a wedge, I reckon we can do it,' I tell him hopefully. I don't dare mention the creek, but I'm sure he's aware of it. I don't want to accept it myself.

As he walks away, I pull the sleeping bag in tighter around my waist. It's soaking wet now, its own weight tugging it off me under the water. The rain has increased ten-fold, into a torrential downpour, and the sound of rushing water is getting louder by the minute as the level rises.

Geert seems gone forever, but when he returns it's with another young sapling that he's cracked by swinging from it and uprooting it. For another hour, we struggle in vain, Geert splashing around in the shin deep water, using the lever while I fumble at piling the stones. They are under water now and my hands are freezing. I try to drive home a stone that is now under the surface, but it's hopeless. We've both run out of energy, drained by our efforts, the rain destroying our spirits completely.

We can't move it; it's too heavy. The thought comes crashing down on my head like a ton of bricks. *I'm trapped.*

Head down, eyes squeezed tightly shut, not wanting to hear myself say what must be said:

'You're gonna have to walk out mate, as soon as it gets light.'

THE DECISION

I felt so strange. Up until now I'd been trying to convince myself that I wasn't that badly hurt, that I was just trapped and I'd probably be fine as soon as I could get out of here. Out from under the rock, out of the creek and up onto the slab under the tarp where it was nice and dry.

Christ, I could see it from where I was pinned; it was only three metres away but it might as well have been three hundred. I imagined dragging myself over to the tarp, trailing two broken legs behind me, and curling up in my sleeping bag to sleep. Falling asleep and praying when I woke it would all just have been a bad dream.

I'd always thought that, in a situation like this — an accident far from immediate medical help, I'd rather be the one that's injured than the guy left to carry out a rescue — the person who was going to have to pull out all stops and take responsibility for another person's well-being, or worse still, their very survival. Mainly because I know how much of a mission I would put myself on, having to get out in a hurry for help. Trying so hard to move as fast as you can whilst being in control enough to not stuff it up, to operate within your limits. *How wrong I had been! What a wanker!* I'd never been badly injured before, not even at home, so how could I have even made that comparison?

Geert had one hell of a journey in front of him, and I knew he was far from looking forward to it. He'd found it difficult on the way up, with all the boulder hopping and bush bashing; most of his life's hiking had been done on well-marked trails. As well, the creek bed had been dry on the way up; now, the entire boulder strewn gully was like an ice skating rink — each and every step would require absolute concentration. Conditions like this are so mentally exhausting, leaving you prone to mistakes, your heart skipping a beat every time you lose traction, unable to do anything but wait for the fall and hope it doesn't hurt too much. Something as easily acquired as a sprained ankle now could be the difference between life and death. It was only just beginning to dawn on me how much I was going to be relying for my very survival on this guy I had only met the day before.

'Mate, you're going to have to be so careful. You have got to make it out, or I'm history!'

Sitting down next to me now, his arm reassuringly around my shoulder as pelting rain poured down our faces and soaked both of us to the skin, Geert reminded me of the story he'd told earlier over our tortellini dinner. A story of how Peter, a friend he'd first met in Nepal, had comforted him through a terrifying night in the Pyrenees mountains.

They had been caught in a storm high on the range bordering

France and Spain. Somewhere along the way they'd lost the poles for the tent. Using their packs inside to create a space, then rocks around the outer edge to tension the nylon, they managed to protect themselves from what turned into a snowstorm. Water ran freely under the tent and it wasn't long before they were both soaking wet. Geert, recovering from a recent injury, was unfit, the cold affecting him more than his companion. Peter worked all night to keep him warm, massaging him and feeding him warm soup, holding him close to keep him warm. Peter had saved Geert's life that night, and it had obviously affected him deeply. His appreciation for Peter's actions shone through in his attention to me now, stroking my shoulders, reassuring me. I responded gratefully, feelings of awkwardness at Geert's affection diminishing as quickly as they had appeared. I squeezed his hand in appreciation, the floodgates behind my eyes threatening to burst.

'You can do it, Warren. You're going to be OK. We can get you through this. People have survived much worse situations than this.'

Have they? I don't know about that.

Though the rain had eased slightly, the level of water around my hips had not. 'Christ, I'm getting cold.'

'OK, mate, do you have some more clothes?' he asked, standing.

'In my pack, there's a bag with another shirt. And some socks,' I replied. He returned with the bag, plus my Therm-a-rest (a thin, lightweight inflatable mattress). I'd made up my bed earlier, getting some satisfaction out of preparing to sleep on a bed of stone. I can add this to my collection of great Therm-a-rest campsite stories, I thought.

Still finding it difficult to accept my position, I watched as Geert crossed the creek to the tarp. Never had anything seemed so near and yet so far. He returned quickly with the Therm-a-rest, the only other shirt I had with me, and a pair of socks. I pulled on the shirt over my woollen vest, then the Gore-Tex back over the top. Geert wrapped the stuff-sack around my right foot, now under water. The socks, I wore as gloves to try to keep my hands warm. They were already numb from the cold, even though I had kept rubbing them vigorously. Geert reorganised my sleeping bag, wrapping it tightly around my waist as the current tried to drag it downstream. Luckily, it was an old bag, bought before down bag manufacturers had discovered Dry Loft (a Gore-Tex covering), so it was filled with Dacron. Dacron is a synthetic material that still manages to retain some warmth even when wet, whereas down bags become a wet, soggy, cold lump.

All right, this is as good as it's going to get warmth wise.

I now wore every item of clothing I had brought, and constantly had to readjust the waterlogged sleeping bag to keep the cold water from flowing straight through it.

Geert then set about collecting branches, some of which had been tossed aside earlier after failing as levers. Setting them in place behind my back, he made them into just the kind of support I needed. This back rest allowed me to sit, as opposed to either lying back, completely in the water, or slumping forward over the slab. Once satisfied, Geert lay the Therm-a-rest across the support, increasing my comfort tremendously.

We began to formulate a plan. Geert would leave at first light, not a minute before. Walking back down in the dark would be suicidal and we both knew that my life now depended on his getting out. It was imperative that he descend with maximum care. Even something as minor as a twisted ankle could turn this situation into even more of a nightmare than it already was.

We both knew it would take at least eight hours for Geert to get back to the nearest campsite, at Little Ramsay Bay, where he would be greeted at the very least by a long drop toilet and a metal food locker, and at best by some fellow hikers. If he did run into other hikers, he would have to decide, depending on their number and experience, whether to send someone back up to me. Or he could send them on in his place to raise the alarm. The trip down would surely take its toll: it may be quicker to send someone fresher in his place. I prayed silently that he would be up to the challenges that lay ahead. I was filled with the sense of dread that, whatever happened, it was totally out of my control.

For now, Geert had to get some rest. He'd need every ounce of energy he could muster tomorrow, and then some. Tomorrow he faced the most demanding and dangerous walk he'd ever undertaken. Right now he was exhausted. I watched him crawl under the tarp into his warm, dry sleeping bag, sensing his feelings of guilt as he called out to me across that small but immeasurable distance, 'Are you all right Warren?'

'Yeah mate! I'm all right!' I replied, my voice raised so as to be heard above the drumming of rain that had begun again in earnest.

ESCAPE FROM PARADISE

As I threw my pack and boots into the car that Sunday afternoon, I felt more alive than I had in weeks. Living in Airlie Beach was hard work. Working as a painter, I had just finished my second month-long contract on Hayman Island. All the contractors worked hard on Hayman, and they partied even harder. I'd left the island a physical wreck, and took a full week to start feeling normal again. I'd been riding the roller coaster that is life in the Whitsundays for seven months now, escaping periodically into the Conway National Park or one of the less inhabited islands for a reality check. It was time to clear my head, get myself back down to earth after living the high life in top gear. I'd heard a fair bit about Hinchinbrook Island over the years. And now seemed like the right time to go and check it out.

Having scribbled a quick note to my new flat mates, I couldn't get out the door fast enough. There's something about a road trip that I find really attractive. Just getting up and going, having no fixed destination. The romance of the road, they call it. The spirit of adventure. I'd been living a fairly nomadic existence for a long time now. I tend to become restless if life becomes too boring. And, for better or worse, I'd made the discovery many moons ago that it's usually only excuses we make up for ourselves that keep us from doing what we really want to do. I'd lost my fear of the unknown and had grown to enjoy the feeling of throwing my cards into the air to see what adventure they'd lead me to when they landed.

Pulling out on to the highway just out of Proserpine, I felt ten foot tall — stereo cranking, endless canefields blurring past the open windows on either side. The hot air lashed my face, keeping the sweat at bay. As the sun sank quickly into the horizon (as it does in North Queensland), the first stars began to speckle the sky. *Free again at last!*

Hours passed as I chewed up kilometre after kilometre of bitumen, headlights blazing the trail ahead of me. It's a strange experience driving at night on an unfamiliar road — the countryside a mystery that won't be revealed till dawn.

Approaching Townsville, I was puzzled by the red lights high in the sky forming a ring around the glowing town below. At first I thought they were aircraft. *Yeah, right!* Once I realised they were beacons on top of hills, I pictured the range surrounding the town, a picture I'm yet to confirm.

I pulled off the road about an hour north of Townsville, happy with the distance I'd covered so far. Clearing a space in the back of the van I rolled out my Therm-a-rest, then left it to self-inflate while I stepped out for a slash. 'Look at those stars!' I couldn't help remarking to myself. 'We love it up here.' I climbed back into the van and fell asleep to the hum of highway traffic and the mosquitoes that had just found me.

Queensland is such a laid back place to travel. Half an hour north of Ingham, just before Cardwell, I took a turn-off to Five Mile Creek. I'm not sure why; it just seemed like a good idea at the time. Waiting for me at the end of a short gravel road was one of the best little swimming holes I've yet found so close to a highway. Places like this are usually tucked away.

With crystal clear water running over the smooth pebbled bottom, it was no more than two metres deep but perfect for that wake-up swim in the morning. I left my clothes where they fell and dived off the bank, skin tingling in anticipation of the water's touch. I love that shudder that you get when you hit cold water; it courses through your whole body like a delicate electric shot, rejuvenating every cell. Swimming under the palms on the opposite bank, I smiled to myself. *It doesn't get much better than this.*

Arriving in Cardwell later that morning, I discovered that, yes, there would be a ferry leaving for Hinchinbrook Island today — in about fifteen minutes. The prospect of rushing into an organisational frenzy at such short notice didn't really appeal to me. Instead, I decided to drive further north for the day and explore the area around Mission Beach.

Back in Cardwell in time for breakfast the next morning, I hit the local supermarket for provisions to last me a week. After parking my car behind the ferry booking office, I stepped on to the boat with a full pack and settled back into my seat, ready to enjoy the smooth ride across Missionary Bay to the island. I kept to myself the whole trip, soaking up the splendour of just being on the water, gazing in awe at the rugged peaks cutting into the horizon. No sooner had the boat moored than I shouldered my pack and left the others swimming at the first beach we reached. The rest of the day I spent walking alone along the spectacular coast, the track at times taking me inland, dropping into rainforest filled gullies before returning me to a new bay each time.

Arriving at Little Ramsay Bay in the afternoon, I was greeted by the sight of a guy sitting on the sand, naked except for his headband, sketching the ocean scene before him. He looked completely relaxed and engrossed in his work, so I didn't greet him. Instead, I dropped my pack from my tired shoulders, stripped off and waded into the cool water for my first swim of the day.

Later, in the cool shade of the umbrella-like Callophyllums that dotted the dune, my neighbour introduced himself as Geert van Keulen. He told me of his plan to climb to the summit of Mount Bowen, the island's highest peak, and had me interested immediately. I'd been admiring the rugged range forming the backbone of the island while swimming earlier, and began calculating whether I could make the climb and still reach my scheduled ferry pick-up at the island's southern end on time.

'Give me ten minutes to think about it,' I told him, but I had already made up my mind.

Waking on the beach before dawn, from the comfort of my sleeping bag I watched the sun begin to rise. There's something almost magical about watching the sun rise over the ocean, the way the first rays arc skyward from the horizon, while the glow of colour spreads towards you across the water. I lay transfixed for a while, then wormed my way out of the bag.

I stretched fully, right down to my toes, and allowed my whole body to soak up the golden rays till I could resist the urge no longer. Walking naked across the smooth, wet sand, I felt my skin crawl with both anticipation and dread as the next wave rushed to greet me. Cool water flowed around my ankles. Stepping in further until the sea swelled around my thighs, I dived straight ahead into the next wave, staying under for a few seconds, savouring the exhilaration as my body kick-started into life. There's nothing better than waking up like that ... well, almost nothing. When you've started the day with a dip in the ocean, you can do anything.

I swam for another ten minutes before leaving the water and having a stretch back on the beach. The sunlight had hit the tops of the peaks now and was spreading slowly down the slopes. I couldn't get over how beautiful these mountains were — Mount Bowen, and 'the thumb' alongside, glowing gold. Geert was up now, so we had breakfast together before re-packing our gear, both keen to get moving. *OK, let's get amongst it!*

Following the track notes Geert had picked up in Townsville, we crossed the lagoon behind camp and made our way upstream until it narrowed into a creek. We found it much easier going in the bush on the northern side at first. It had been cleared somewhat by a recent fire, so a lot of the tangly scrub was gone. But it didn't stay that way for long.

Soon we were forced back into the creek bed, ducking under branches and jumping from rock to rock. Geert was finding it a lot tougher than I was. I found myself stopping and waiting a lot, trying not to get too far ahead. It's much harder walking at a slower pace than your usual, and I found it difficult to stick with the 'slowest sets the pace' rule. With this sort of walking you need to build up a momentum if you're going to travel quickly and efficiently. Moving slowly and stopping to balance after each move actually uses more energy. I tried to stay behind Geert as much as possible, letting him set the pace, but soon found myself back in front. After a couple of hours or so we stopped for a break, firing up the Trangia (a compact fuel stove) for a coffee.

'How are you travelling mate?' I asked Geert.

'I'm finding it difficult to keep my balance. I've already fallen a couple of times back there.'

'You'll be right. Just take it easy. We're not in a big hurry. The notes say five hours but if it takes us a bit more, it won't matter.'

I'd rarely felt more confident on my feet, bounding from rock to rock fearlessly, almost gracefully. It took me quite by surprise really. I hadn't carried a full pack any distance for at least eight or nine months and fully expected to take a couple of days to find my feet completely.

It's always hard to judge walking times as described in track notes;

everybody's got a different idea on what a steady pace is, or how fast an experienced walker covers different terrain. I knew we certainly weren't going to break any records but figured we must be round about halfway to the campsite, which I presumed to be no more than a cleared space big enough to put up a tent. From there it should be an hour or so bouldering to the summit, leaving us with time to retrace our steps back to Little Ramsay Bay by late tomorrow afternoon.

We set off again, the sun high in the sky now, beating down on us through the canopy. In places water tumbled from one boulder to another. The further we went, the larger the boulders became, making for bigger and bigger pools. Unable to resist the temptation of another swim, I stripped off and eased into the cold mountain stream, taking a quick breath before plunging my head under. *Now this is what I call living!*

Geert arrived and sat on a rock beside the pool. I swam across to a small waterfall on the other side, pulling myself over slippery rocks while the force of the water tried to push me back. *No way*, I thought. *I'm going under there.* Behind the sheet of water was a space where the rock cut under. I pushed myself through the screen, water pounding my neck and shoulders, finding I could breathe on the other side!

'Have a go mate, it's excellent.'

I had that exhilarating feeling of being in the wild, of being totally immersed in nature. This is what I'd come for — not so much to *see* the sights, but to *feel* them, to *be part of* them.

I slipped out of the water, treading carefully with my wet feet, then sat on a rock in the sun to dry off while Geert took my place. It was just what he needed: a bit of enjoyment, time out from the demanding walk to appreciate where we were and why we were here.

We continued for another hour before stopping for lunch.

'How much further do you think it is Warren?' Geert questioned.

'It's hard to say, but I don't think we could be more than an hour away now.' It was about 1.00pm, so we'd been travelling for nearly five hours. 'We must be pretty bloody close.'

As we got higher, the creek narrowed, forcing us to crouch under the low branches reaching for their brothers on the other side to form a canopy. Several times we encountered a fork in the path where another stream joined ours. Some were just the rejoining point for our creek after a brief separation upstream. Others had begun separately, only now joining together for the journey to the sea. Most of these junctions had been clearly marked with rock cairns by walkers who'd passed before us. Until I came to a junction with no guiding signs whatsoever.

What's the story, we couldn't have passed the campsite, could we? Could I have just walked past it? And Geert also?

The gully had filled with shadows as the sun dipped lower into the hills ahead of us. It was getting fairly late now, Geert was looking pretty anxious, probably wondering what the hell he'd got himself into. *Why on earth would anyone want to do this sort of thing for fun?*

I was starting to feel anxious myself now. We should have reached our destination. If we'd gone off track, we wouldn't have time to back-track and try to find the right way. I had to be on the ferry at the south end of the island on Saturday, Geert on Sunday. Besides, I hadn't come across a spot big enough to put a tent up yet, all of the scrub so far closing right in on both sides. I decided to climb out of the gully to get a better view and see which would be the most likely direction to follow.

Struggling through waist high heath, trying to gain height when my feet weren't even touching the ground, I scrambled to the top of a heath-covered rocky outcrop. Majestic peaks rose all around me, providing an amazing view. Although I was standing on the top of this small rise I didn't have enough height to work out which course to follow. *Right or left?*

Neither looked good, so I picked right. Leaving my pack with Geert, I made my way up through what was now a very overgrown gully with a trickle of water running through it. I battled on for another couple of hundred metres with no sign of a cairn, before returning to Geert. *We couldn't be in the wrong gully, could we?*

'It must be up this way mate,' I motioned to the left as I joined Geert back at the fork.

I kept moving as he donned his pack to follow. I was desperate to find something now; I didn't want to let him down, to give him any doubt about my ability to deal with the situation. I wanted to forge ahead and return with the good news that all was well, the campsite was just upstream.

Bounding from rock to rock, I stopped often, scanning the scene for a cairn or some other sign. Half a kilometre upstream I came across a large, flat slab of rock, sloping into, and forming part of, the river bed, which was dry at the moment but looked like it wouldn't stay that way if the water level rose. (Another golden rule, never camp in a river bed.) *It's far from ideal*, I thought, *but if worse comes to worst, this will have to do for an emergency campsite. If it does rain, and the river rises significantly, we'll just have to break camp and sit up in the heath for the night. We won't get much sleep, but that won't kill us.*

Waiting for Geert to arrive, I became increasingly pissed off with myself at the realisation that we may not be where we were supposed to be.

Are you really enjoying this? I asked myself. In a way, I was. Being caught out like this reinforces your confidence as a bushwalker. It reminds you that, no matter what happens, you can survive. Take away another comfort — the campsite, in this case — and you'll still be OK. But we were running out of time.

'All right mate, it's getting late. We're just going to have to make do with whatever space we can find to string up a tarp,' I told Geert as he approached.

'This isn't the campsite?' he asked despairingly.

'No, it's not, mate. We should have come across it by now, though. I don't know what's happened. We must have taken a wrong fork somewhere. I can't see how, but I can't think of any other explanation,' I said, almost apologetically. 'If you wait here, I'm going to check a bit further upstream, just to make sure we're not just around the corner from it.' There's nothing worse than setting up camp late in the day, or at night, in a really horrible spot, only to find in daylight that you've camped within cooee of where you were supposed to be.

'OK' was his brief reply as he flung the pack from his shoulders.

'If I don't find anything upstream, we're going to have to camp here, mate, on this slab. I know it doesn't look too appealing, but it's the only piece of open flat ground I've seen all day. I won't be long.'

With that, I took off upstream, feeling oh so light without my pack. Bouncing from rock to rock like a gazelle, concentrating on my feet, I rarely glanced more than a few metres ahead.

Less than ten minutes later, I became aware of a splashing, trickling sound in the distance, like a waterfall. It grew louder and louder until, as I climbed out of a very narrow gully, overgrown from both sides, I found myself standing in the shadow of a huge rock wall, a thirty to forty metre vertical face.

'Jesus! Where the hell did that come from?' I asked, aloud.

I'd been so concerned with my footwork that I hadn't even seen it coming. It towered above me, and spread completely across my path, almost a hundred metres across. A band of water flowed down the centre of the face above me, a trickle rather than a waterfall, just enough to keep the moss growing. I began scouring for some kind of route, some trace of a potential way around, but this was the end of the road as far as the stream was concerned. The way both left and right led into dense scrub. Without the benefit of a gully to follow, I was soon forced back to the cliff base. It was too steep to climb, and, especially with the whole thing looking damp, it appeared totally impassable. *This couldn't possibly be the way*. The track notes didn't mention any technical climbing. Besides, it was too late in the day to go any higher, too late to be looking for another campsite while we had the slab to fall back on.

I made my way back to Geert to give him the bad news.

RAIN

Head bowed, I shifted my weight often, trying to get some relief from the steady, throbbing pain. It wasn't the sharp, burning pain I'd first endured. Rather a deep, cold, throbbing like you get after hitting your thumb with a hammer. Every time I moved to rearrange myself, which was often, Geert called out again. 'Are you OK, mate? Hang in there, you're going to be all right!'

Sleep was impossible to come by for both of us. There was no way Geert could sleep, with me in the situation I was in. For me, the very concept of sleep was ridiculous. The rain continued coming down in bucketfuls while I tried every position possible to get some relief from the discomfort in my legs. I felt like some kind of outcast, banished from the camp by an act of God.

Only now can I appreciate how Geert felt, huddled in his warm sleeping bag while I lay slumped over the slab in the rain. He must have felt utterly useless; I know I would have. Every five to ten minutes he'd call out, 'Are you all right Warren?'

'Yeah,' I'd reply, above the din of the rain.

Well, I was, to the extent that either of us could do anything about it. It was almost as if I was trying to put myself in a state of suspended animation, trying to blank out of existence the time between now and sunrise, not wanting to live it at all. I don't believe in willing the future towards me. Wishing time to pass faster than it already does is a sin I've been guilty of — but that's what it is, a sin. Ideally, we should all live for the moment, because that's the only certainty. Time is precious and every second should be appreciated and enjoyed as if it's your last. That's my theory, anyway. I don't practise it myself but I envy the few people I know who do. But now, with the rain and the cold and the fear, time could not pass quickly enough.

Engine!

'Geert! Plane!' The droning sound is unmistakable, even above the rain. The rush of adrenaline lifts me, my eyes scanning the sky for some kind of confirmation.

'Quick, mate! We need a fire!' Geert is out of his bag in an instant, scanning the sky for the source of the sound before scrambling off in search of something to burn.

'It's all soaking wet, Warren!'

'It doesn't matter, it'll burn!' adding, as he frantically snatches up kindling, 'There's a candle in my pack, in the front pocket. Use it under the small twigs, it'll take a while but it should get it going!' Using a candle to light a fire is a skill I picked up in Tasmania while campaigning in the Tarkine. It gets so wet in there, you almost need to be able to light a fire underwater.

Geert gets it all together quickly for someone who hasn't used this method of fire lighting before, but the wet kindling is still spitting and hissing in objection as the low hum disappears into the night. It may not even have passed overhead; neither of us has seen any lights.

Geert persevered with the fire for another five minutes or so, but it was a lost cause. On one hand, I desperately wanted Geert to get the fire going, to keep it alight just in case another plane flew over. But it would be such a long shot. I was working on the theory that, because fires are not allowed on the island, it would have been noticed and possibly read as a distress signal. But, unless the occupants were familiar with the area (and they wouldn't have even been able to make out the island in the dark otherwise) and with the rule of no fires, then our attempt at a signal would appear as nothing more than a campfire. Was it worth having Geert up all night keeping a fire going, when he was going to need all of his resources in the morning?

Geert knew I'd been clutching at straws, but he didn't say anything. He made his way back towards the shelter of the tarp as I slumped back over the slab, both our spirits dampened after a faint glimmer of hope.

The drumming of steady rain on the hood of my jacket became louder, forcing my mind away from thoughts of rescue to the stark reality rising all around me. With my head in my hands, eyes squeezed tightly shut behind my palms, my mind raced like a roulette wheel while I prayed for the little silver ball not to stop where I knew it would.

The water level was now above my waist.

THE DEAFENING ROAR

'Geert!'

'Are you all right, mate?' His reply is immediate.

'Mate, we've got to try again. I've got to get out!'

'Hang on!' he shouts back above the rain, stepping into the rapid flow and quickly splashing towards me.

'The river's coming up! I've got to get out!'

I'd been sitting there, feeling it rise, not wanting to accept that it was really happening until I couldn't stand it any more. The trickle down the buttress upstream now sounded as though a dam had burst: a roaring torrent cascaded out of the darkness. The fact that I couldn't see it made it all the more terrifying. I half expected one huge wave to surge forward and completely engulf me. That would have made it a lot easier. Instead, I was sitting right in the middle of its path, trapped, as it slowly rose.

I'm going to drown!

Geert looks scared. 'What the hell do you want me to do, Warren?'

'We've got to try again,' I gasp, almost pleading. 'I can't stay under here, I'm finished if I don't get out!' Reaching under the shelf, I try to position the pillar of stones so they're standing more squarely on top of each other.

'I need more rocks mate, not so round,' and Geert's off, splashing in the knee deep water, to see what he can find. My hands are freezing as I work underwater, trying to pull off the balancing act required.

Fear keeps rising in my throat. I'm doing everything in my power to stop me from just crying out and howling. From falling into a sobbing heap and giving up. *No! I can't die like this!* I shudder, then feel my own anger at myself for almost giving in. *I have to stay in control!*

Regardless of what you believe about drowning, whether or not it's the peaceful death some claim it to be, the position I was in was more terrifying than I could have ever imagined. I'd been faced with the possibility of drowning before, while snorkelling. I'd been held under a 'bommy' for what seemed like minutes before being released and sent kicking and clawing the water in my dash to the surface. But that was all over in less than a minute. *I could be here like this for hours before the water slowly rises above my head.*

As if I'm not cold enough already, the thought chills me to the bone. My head fills with vivid images of water splashing around my face as I crane my neck to get clear. *What will happen? Will I just hold my breath till I pass out, or will I be gulping in water, trying to breathe and choking, gasping in water and retching again until I just seize up and die?*

Geert returns with more rocks, piling them up in front of me to form a dam.

'It's all right, mate, I don't think it will come up much higher,' he tries to assure me, but I'm looking at the bank.

Why not? It has before. I can see by the light of the torch the telltale signs indicating previous water levels, and it doesn't look good. *The marks are above my head!* My head is spinning. *What's the frame of my pack made of?* The frame of my last pack was made from aluminium tubing, but I don't think this one is. If I could find a piece of tubing, I could use it like a straw to breathe air from the surface when I go under. But how long could I last doing that? I'm already freezing. Geert's still piling up the stones while I keep smashing away at the wedge stone. It's under the water level now, though, and I can't strike with full force. Eventually, through exhaustion, I have to stop. Geert does the same. My situation has become so desperate, the only way I can deal with it is to accept it, slumping over the slab in submission. I'm stuffed.

So this is it, hey — this is how the story ends? Although Geert's right beside me, I'm no longer strongly aware of his presence. Withdrawing into myself, having given up any hope of survival, I begin to see myself as a character in some kind of bizarre movie. Almost like I am watching myself from afar. *Will I get to watch myself die like this?*

Am I imagining things or has the rain eased off? It has!

Geert senses it also, coming back to life with me. Is this a reprieve? Or is it just a prelude to the next stage, the next twist that even the most ardent of art-house movie fans would struggle to pick. Geert's rubbing my shoulders in encouragement.

'It's stopping, mate. The rain is stopping.'

I'm having trouble sharing his enthusiasm, not yet willing to venture back out into the world that's been turned upside down on me. I just want to cry with relief, but I can't. That would mean accepting that everything out there is all right, and it isn't. I felt much safer inside, preferring to peek out from under my dripping but now silent hood.

It is true. The rain has stopped.

But will that stop the river rising? We're very close to the summit, so the response should be fairly quick. Or is that just wishful thinking?

Water is still roaring over the wall upstream, though it doesn't seem so formidable without the rain as a backdrop. As the anxiety gradually recedes, the throbbing pain returns to the forefront of my thoughts. *My legs! My legs are killing me!*

Geert comforts me as I rock back and forward, trying to tense my legs to gain relief. 'You're going to be all right Warren. You're a tough bastard. You're gonna make it.'

I nod in agreement, 'I know. I have to.'

We agree to have one more try first thing in the morning, as soon as it gets light. If that doesn't work, Geert walks out for help. As he leaves me again, I sense his reluctance to do so, but he has no choice. He has to get some more rest, and there can only be a few more hours of darkness left. I watch him cross to the promised land once more, then turn my attention back to blocking out the pain. Trying hard not to think about the hours that lie ahead before daylight.

I've seen quite a few sunrises in my time but this must be the longest in the history of the planet. I watch as the sky slowly begins to lighten to the east — so agonisingly slowly that it seems at times that nothing is happening, as if time has come to a standstill. That on this day, of all days, the sun will not rise.

Until, ever so slowly, the lightening sky begins to spread its glow, silhouettes becoming three-dimensional objects.

How long should I wait before yelling out to Geert? I don't have to wait long for the answer. I am relieved to hear movement as he climbs out of his bag.

'Are you OK, mate?' he calls.

'Yeah, I'm all right.' Which is far from true, but, considering the circumstances, I suppose I am. 'Are you ready to go again, mate?' I add, knowing that time is critical now, and we have time for only one attempt before Geert has to leave. Otherwise he risks running out of daylight and that will be the end of me.

This has to work, I plead to myself. All I can think about is getting out. I force the other outcome from my mind, not even wanting to contemplate it. Geert heaves on the sapling lever while I use a hammerstone and wedge. *Even if we could lift it a fraction at a time…* For half an hour we battle on, refusing to give up. As Geert pulls down on the lever with all his might, I drive the wedge in frantically. I am desperate to gain even the slightest reprise from the crushing weight, but nothing moves. I realise now that, when we moved it last night, we just helped it settle in to its final resting place. It is painfully obvious what has to happen.

'Mate, you've got to make it out.' Almost begging him, feeling the acid rise in my throat, hearing the fear in my own voice.

Geert nods, 'Don't you worry. I'm going to get you out of here.'

He sets about packing up — first his gear, then mine. He collects items of mine that he thinks I am going to need while he's gone. In three separate plastic bags, he gives me a torch, my first aid kit and half a loaf of rye bread, some paw-paw spears, a small bag of dried fruit and nuts, a piece of sweaty cheese, a plastic mug, a blue polyurethane tarp, and my diary with a pen. He ties all three bags together with a piece of cord then slings that over my head, resting the bags on the rock in front of me like a fold-down tray in an aeroplane. The cord around my neck will stop the bags being washed away if I fall asleep or the river rises up over the rock.

Saying goodbye to Geert is one of the strangest and scariest things I've ever done. I do everything but beg him to be careful, insisting that it doesn't matter how long it takes him, he just has to make it.

'Stay in the bush alongside the creek if you can. It will be way too slippery in amongst the rocks, mate, and if you slip, we could both be goners.' I hold back from stressing my concerns too strongly for fear of making him freak out any more than he already must be. I don't want to put him under any more pressure than he is already under. But I am terrified. We both know how hard he found it yesterday, but neither of us mentions it. He has to go with my confidence in him, as well as his own in himself.

We go through the plan again. He will build a fire on the beach as soon as he arrives. If there are enough people at the camp, and they have the experience, he will send them up to me.

I take his hand, then hug him tightly, fighting back the tears. 'I reckon I can last tonight, mate. But,' my voice straining, almost breaking up, 'I don't know if I can stand another one.'

With that, he stands up, lifts his pack and slings it over one shoulder, then feeds the other arm through. It feels like I am watching him in slow motion as he adjusts his pack and faces me one more time.

'Take it easy mate, you can do it,' I say as I grip his hand, then let go.

'I'll see you soon, Warren,' he replies before turning and taking the first steps of his journey. We have known each other for only a few days, but I feel lonelier than ever before as I watch him walk away.

GEERT VAN KEULEN: **Planning the trip**

After completing the Overland trek and the even more magnificent South West Coast trek in Tasmania, I flew north over a lot of good Australian walking areas, a very satisfied and relaxed man.

In Tasmania I had been able to fulfil the main purpose of my vacation to Australia: to hike for about a month in the spectacular wilderness, unwinding from the stresses that I had brought with me from Europe, without the big crowds; trying to get my head screwed back on properly — a spiritual refuelling. Doing these two treks in windswept and rainy conditions not only strengthened me physically, causing me to lose seven kilograms in weight, but also improved my mental health a great deal. I had gained many experiences, filled two sketchbooks with watercolours and one notebook with text, and ended up with a damaged camera, which I had dropped in the Southern Ocean while photographing bull kelp on the first day!

My northern destination was Townsville, where I intended to stay one month with Rohan Bastin, a very good friend who teaches at James Cook University. When I was planning my Australian trip back in the Netherlands, he had told me over the phone about a spectacular hike on Hinchinbrook Island, a protected tropical island between Townsville and Cairns, close to the Great Barrier Reef.

With Rohan's minimal but promising information in mind I chatted to a few bushwalkers from Queensland with whom I shared a campsite somewhere on the Tasmanian coast, eager to take in as much valuable information as possible about Hinchinbrook. It was the day before I crossed the notorious Ironbound Ranges, a mountain range that can be dangerous as the weather there is very unpredictable. In the cold Tasmanian evening, these Queenslanders told me about the hike in the tropics, about the challenging walk to the summit of Mount Bowen, the spectacular scenery that I was going to be rewarded with on the top, looking out over the Pacific, the Hinchinbrook Channel and the mainland. Not a bad prospect.

In Townsville I paid $300 to have the camera repaired — apparently the inside looked a bit like a small salt mine bordered by sand dunes! In the second week I visited the National Parks office and asked a park ranger on duty what I could expect in climbing Mount Bowen — what kind of wildlife I would come across, what kind of vegetation, would it be all right to camp up there and would there be enough drinking water?

As we chatted along, comparing each other's hiking experiences, he told me it would be all right to go alone, even though the guidelines required a minimum party of three trekkers. He judged my experiences in the south west of Tasmania as sound and supplied me with a one-week trekking permit. I could do the trek in three or four days but I intended to take my time. He gave me photocopies of track notes written by other hikers (which he said he wasn't supposed to do).

With the permit and notes in my wallet I descended on the biggest super-market I could find and bought a pile of nice food. Much more deluxe than the muesli and instant mashed potatoes I had eaten in Tassie. I said good-bye to Rohan and Trish and hit the road. A Greyhound bus took me to Cardwell, stop-off place for the boat trip to the island.

Cardwell demanded that all visitors who passed through the place were aware of the conflict that was current at that time. I could feel the tension there.

Diary: I believe that Queensland is much more conservative than Tasmania. At least most of the Tassies understand they walk on precious and unique soil these days. Here all emphasis is thrown on developing. Lovers of nature and environmentalists are not really desired in the place. Cardwell is a town where a developer is going to build a marina. He already has damaged two Barrier Reef islands with his developments and now another one is on the cards. The world-famous Hinchinbrook Channel separates Hinchinbrook Island from the mainland. The island, but not its channel, is very well protected by a World Heritage listing. No building is allowed on the island. So Mr Developer is going to build his resort right oppo-site the island, on the beaches of the channel. The precious marine life, the dugongs, tortoises, fish and micro marine life will be forever chased away by powerboats, jet skis and more of those toys of smell and noise, and the island will thus be damaged little by little.

When the big bus rolled into town we were welcomed by, on the one hand, huge signs declaring Cardwell the best place on earth and, on the other, signs such as: 'YES MARINA, YES JOBS, YES RESORT'. Small businesses typically all had signs in their front yards!

One of the dilemmas of nature conservation is that often people from the outside have to notice or take action. I was waiting for the ferry, sitting on the floor of the jetty, casually leaning against my pack in the early warmth of the day. Overlooking the beautiful channel I thought about these unfortunate environmental issues.

Setting off

It was a short but lovely trip. Dugongs and tortoises came up for air all around us, and shiny fish called 'long toms' skittered over the water. The boat found a channel in the dense mangrove forests and took us to a small jetty, from where a boardwalk led through the mangroves towards more solid ground. Mud crabs watched and heard us make our way over it.

I strolled off the jetty, away from the other two trekkers and onto the beach to look for fossils, which I found at the flood line: tiny fossilised crayfish. I sketched the scenery in front of me, which was a lot different to the drama of Tassie: blue skies and a long white sandy beach, not interrupted by rocks but edged by palm trees and tropical vegetation.

This was going to be a slow, hippie style trek for me. I had a couple of fantastic days and nights, swimming in the nude, walking alone on the tropical beach and feasting on exciting meals. I read a few good books on meditation. I painted my watercolours with quite a different palette than I'd used on Tasmania, and in the comfortable warmth they dried a lot quicker too. I thought of the past experiences in my hectic job that had nearly driven me crazy and what I was going to do about it when I returned home. Being away from it all allowed me to reorganise myself mentally for Europe. It put quite a different perspective on things

Diary: Nina Bay, Tuesday, April 7th. Mosquito coils slowly burn up in the sand around me, leaving spots of ashes in circles on the ground. Above my head the Southern Cross stands in an indigo sky, surrounded by millions of stars. My tent has not been aired for a week, so I've left its two entrances open, allowing the fumes of the bush and my body odour to get out into the warm evening air. I am relaxed and feel great. The first couple of days in Queensland were a bit hectic — getting used to the significant difference in temperature, and talking so much with my friends. But now, I'm on the beach of a tropical, unpopulated island. No mud, button grass, leeches or frost. Coming to Australia and hiking in Tassie was an excellent idea. The walks took the pressures away and a week on Hinchinbrook Island will take away the last remains of it.

Arriving

On the third afternoon I arrived at Little Ramsay Bay campsite, from which the track leads up to Mount Bowen. Late that afternoon two hikers walked into the camp, an Englishman and an Australian. We came together to eat our meals, sitting around the metal rat-proof storage box — apart from the jetty, the only facilities on the island! (Bush rats keep an eye on the trekker and have the urge to go after their food and rubbish. After dinner I dug a deep hole in the sand to bury my left over pasta. It did not stop them from having a go at it and when I woke up in the morning it had disappeared.) I suggested that the three of us go up the mountain. The Englishman decided that walking the route to the other end of the island provided him with enough challenge and he quickly said 'No'.

The other one decided to think about it. He borrowed my track notes and came to my tent a few hours later. He agreed to join me the following morning. His name was Warren Macdonald. He was 32 years old and from Melbourne. We went over the track notes and Warren told me he was an experienced guide who took environmentalists over non-existing tracks in the Tasmanian wilderness. Deep in the rainforest they held up work while trying to focus media attention on the building of a road through the Tarkine, Tasmania's north-west. Deep in the forest they would try to get coverage of their protest against the building of a road through the north-western Tasmanian bush. Warren was immensely fit and strong and seemed to be a perfect partner for our journey. Most importantly he was blessed with a good sense of humour, which was the icing on the cake. According to the track notes our trip should take six to seven hours.

Diary: The weather on this evening is excellent and I've taken the fly off the tent. Candles create a warm and cosy atmosphere inside it and lying on my Therm-a-rest I listen to the water washing against the shore until it takes me into a fine sleep.

The climb

On Thursday, April 9th, we left our beach camp at 7.30am. I'd left my tent and a lot of other heavy stuff, including food, behind in the storage box. There was a logbook in it and I wrote down our destination and plans. Then I took my pack with just the essentials needed for a few days: plenty of food, a burner, rain clothes and my sketchbook and notebook; plus a lot of enthusiasm and a healthy dose of curiosity. I had put a black and white film in the camera and was on the prowl for challenging photography.

Warren had packed his gear also and decided to take his tarpaulin. Since we were in the tropics there wasn't a need for a tent. Happy to be able to leave a lot of weight behind, we started our trek. We waded through a lagoon and soon found Warrawilla Creek. There was no track as such. A poorly marked path lead up to Mount Bowen over the rocks that were in the creek. Hard yakka! Rock-hopping and cursing at the enormous stones I had to conquer, I went up. It was to be a difficult walk over very rough terrain, winding our way up — now left, now right — seeking out the easiest possible route over the boulders and rocks.

My month of walking experience in Tassie seemed like one day, compared with the level of fitness that Warren displayed. Christ, what a fit bastard. With his long legs he seemed to walk like he was simply going up a stairway instead of a rock loaded creek. Because he was taller than I was he seemed to have more leverage and it seemed he could walk a lot more comfortably than I could. In this terrain, going for a gain in altitude of some 1100 metres is a fair plod.

It was a very humid day. There was a lot of moisture in the air, as it was the end of the rainy season. Most of the time I walked alone. Slipping and sliding and hurting myself a few times when I 'missed' a rock. Some of them had a cover of a slippery substance — a kind of black moss — a little cushioned and providing grip when it was dry, but when wet very treacherous and more slippery than a slide covered in green soap! Many rocks had been eroded into smooth round objects: perfect round boulders, strewn across the creek, as if dropped by an aeroplane.

Once, I slipped away, thrown off balance by a badly 'sitting' pack, and fell in a rock pool. Just able to keep my head dry I got out of the water quick smart and threw off my pack and my camera bag from around my waist. This bag has a centre compartment with the camera in it and two side-pouches for film, lens cleaner, batteries, a pocket knife and a cigarette lighter. Quickly I got out the camera, fearing another disaster like in Tasmania, but the water hadn't penetrated through the material of the bag. Lucky! There was an angel travelling with me. Still, I decided to give it a good clean and continued the climb only after I had stored it away properly. The sun soon burned my naked shoulders and dried my pants.

In another careless moment I fell hard. I looked in front of me and saw Warren easily getting on top of a big rounded rock. 'Obviously he is technically a much better climber than me,' I grumbled under my panting breath. Supported by a healthy dose of Dutch swearing, I approached the rock after deciding to go the same route Warren had taken. But my agility could not touch his. 'Oh well, I still have fun, so I should concentrate on making the best of it,' I thought.

Meanwhile my rucksack did not sit well on my back at all. The poor thing had endured quite a hammering in Tasmania and now the straps, clips, buckles and zips protested angrily at yet another challenge to their strength. Just as I was applying all of my miserable rock climbing technique to try to get up this round, red bastard, and was using my hands and the sides of my walking boots to hold on, my pack decided to pull me sideways. Probably my water bottle shifted from one side to the other in the top compartment of my pack, enough to destroy my balance.

I fell one and a half metres and landed hard on all fours. It hurt badly and I stayed put for a while in the shallow water of the creek, sitting on hands and knees and checking whether I had bruised or broken something. Still in the same position, I unbuckled my pack and let it slide off my back. In Tasmania the zip of the top compartment had been broken and I had stuck a large safety pin in the middle of the hole. Zip fatigue. It was as if the two separated parts were a mouth laughing at me. I looked up to check whether Warren had seen my clumsy ascent but he was not in sight so I got up, cleaned my hands and continued my path once more, sweating not only from the heat but also from fear, exertion and embarrassment.

The hardest part of this type of walking is that you can't build up momentum. A diesel like me wants to keep going. This kind of work is too much stop and standing for me. After each rock, there's another one waiting. Looking around, you continuously have to choose a new pathway. Deep rock pools, small waterfalls and cascades make you zigzag along, frequently switching from one side of the creek to the other.

Often, after yet another bend, I would find Warren sitting or lying on a stone, relaxing, looking up at what was in store for us. Sometimes all I saw on my 'joyous' tropical walk were stones. Having come around the umpteenth bend, I saw Warren's head popping up above a little rock. A round object that grew as I approached it, a red goat beard on the bottom of it, followed by a strong neck that rested on massive shoulders.

Diary: Warren has to be patient with me. I don't like it much when I have to wait for another person frequently. Do I imagine that he is secretly laughing at me or am I being paranoid? I'm sure that the tiredness makes me think less than logically. Warren is too polite and patient to do that. When I reach him we talk and he reckons we are about half an hour away from the top! Now that sounds better.

Diary: We have arrived at a magnificent rock pool and throw off our packs to jump into the ice-cold water. Faaaantastic! We stick our smelly heads and bodies under a small waterfall and play like children, shouting and laughing into the dense bush around us. I take pictures of the creek and of us washing ourselves under the small waterfall. Refreshed, I put my Explorer socks over my red and tired feet, remembering how I bought these socks in Adelaide some 12 years ago, the best Australian product I have ever come across. My mother has repaired them once and I have never had any blisters while walking in them. Usually I wear two pair and since I have covered many kilometres I believe in these socks and have grown fond of them, much to the annoyance of my girlfriend who feels that I'm attached to an ever-growing variation of junk! Then I lace up my German boots. They have *not* lasted 12 years! It's probably going to be the last trip for them. The soles have been renewed once but, like my pack, the Tasmanian conditions have given them a hard time. The surface of the soles has too little texture left for this kind of work but at least they protect my ankles.

As we continued our stroll up the creek I noticed that the temperature was getting very warm. The sweat soon ran over my face and drew traces over my sunglasses. Not long after leaving our sublime rock pool I had not a dry fibre left in my clothes. Treacherously the humidity had got the better of me. Because I had been walking near and sometimes through a creek, sheltered by the lush rainforest on both sides, I did not pay much attention to the weather.

By about 4.00pm the half-hour we thought we were from the top had passed some three hours before. The creek had many side creeks and we realised that we could have taken the wrong one. That didn't worry us. Glad to stop, we threw off our packs at a large flat stone, perhaps six by three metres bordered by scrub and the jungle on one side and about a metre above the creek, gradually sloping down to the creek itself. Warren judged it to be a fine spot for an emergency bivouac in case we didn't feel like going further. I couldn't agree more and planted my bum on the stone. Rubbing my tired calves and massaging a sore right knee. Judging by our own walking experiences and the time of the day, we realised that we should have been on the top of Mount Bowen by now.

While I took a rest, Warren went up a bit further to check out the area and when he came back we decided to put up camp and stop walking. We planned to return the next morning, as we couldn't afford much more time on our trekking permits. Mount Bowen had to wait another time to be visited by either of us.

Warren took his tarpaulin out of his rucksack and made us a comfy camp. Our Therm-a-rests provided excellent comfort against the hard rock where we would sleep. While Warren attached the lines of the tarp to the trees I cooked tortellini, straight out of a packet. Soon the vapour of the cooking pot mixed with the aroma of the rainforest, into the dark sky of the overcast bush. Cooking after a hard day of walking is one of the finest moments; eating it, a close second. The tortellini wasn't good by a long shot but we threw a layer of melted cheddar on top of it, added chillies, garlic and a few slices of salami, and ate it with pleasure. I guess anything would have tasted fine.

Warren started to tell his tales of being a wilderness guide in Tassie. Quite incredible. He told me in fine detail how his friend had a leech stuck out of his eye! And how his mates all panicked while the only woman in the group of tough men had the guts to remove the sucker! These kinds of stories, calmly spoken, drifted into the tropical evening. It was great to be here, I thought, exchanging our explorations and past adventures. A bond was developing between this strong character from Melbourne and me. Although I had only met him the day before, it seemed like I had known him for a very long time. This is chemistry!

It was a great night but at about eight the hard work of the day took its revenge and I felt really cactused. I went for a wee, balancing on the edge of the rock close to where the rock and the creek dropped sharply, a few metres from our tarp. It wasn't possible to walk away from it on a flat stretch of surface and I certainly didn't fancy more rock hopping just to relieve myself! I took my boots off and organised my stuff a little around the camp. I had not had the time or the energy to draw, but took a few photos, using the in-built flash. Sitting on a rock I slowly cleaned my teeth, looking up at the black sky. Clouds only allowed a few stars to shine through its layers. It didn't worry me, as I was too tired to worry about anything anyway.

'I'm going to hit the sack mate,' I said, using my best Australian accent, and crawled under the tarp.

Warren trapped

After checking if everything was in place I tied Warren's torch by its cord to the central tent pole which carried the tarpaulin. My fleece jacket functioned as an excellent pillow and I put my arms under my head, closed my eyes and started to daydream, reflecting on the evening and the day. Never happier, tired but relaxed and content.

Warren was going to do his 'things' and I started to drift off just about straight away. Lying on my back the first dreams started to come when all of a sudden I was woken up by an agonising yell coming from near the creek.

'A torch, quick. Oh fuck, get a torch! GET A TORCH!'

I remember sitting up straight in my sleeping bag, not being sure what was going on and trying to get the torch loose from the bar of the tarpaulin. When I had finally succeeded in doing so — in what seemed an hour but was only a few seconds — I went outside and found Warren lying in the creek, covered by a big slab of rock.

The initial shock was enormous. Then the absurd reality hit me. I was dressed in my underpants and stood next to Warren while he was trapped under the rock. Both of us were barefoot. It was very dark in the rainforest and with Warren's torch I checked his position, quickly scanning the area around him. It didn't look good.

The rock was grey coloured and shaped in a wedge and had come loose from another much larger mother rock. Warren's left leg was completely covered by it and his right bottom leg appeared from the knee down. The knee seemed to swell by the minute. The boulder had trapped him very badly. What if it had covered him even more, damaging his ribcage, or what if it had only damaged a lower part of his body. All kinds of thoughts flashed through my mind.

Warren had been climbing out of the gully, to urinate away from the creek, when the rock, eroded over thousands of years, had finally come loose and come down, Warren half under it. Just above his right knee a sharp fraction of the rock covered his lower thigh and a small part of his upper thigh reappeared before the rest of the boulder covered the thigh up to his waist. His pelvis was also covered by it. With his behind he sat just inside a shallow section of the creek.

About one metre to his left the creek dropped a few metres. Some water streamed behind Warren's back and fell into the depth. There wasn't much water in it at that time. He was also sitting with the middle of his lower body on a small but tough tree. It must have just sat in between his buttocks and came out from behind him.

I cannot remember exactly what my reaction was in the first minutes after his fall.

Soon the reality of the scene became very obvious. Thank God there was no panic! Warren's calmness must have helped a great deal because what would have happened if he had started to scream and yell? He didn't. It allowed me to concentrate on the things that needed to be done. To get him out, to make him feel comfortable and that I probably had to leave him behind to get help tomorrow morning. But the last thought did not return in my mind until many hours had passed when the exhaustion and despair made me snap out of my concentration and adrenaline high.

At first I tried to pull the rock away from him with my hands but it wouldn't move a bit and I felt like I was tearing apart the tissue in my body. Then I started to collect wood. Old and young trees with strong green wood. Warren remained calm after his initial outcry and we decided to try and lever him out from underneath the rock. The trees, young and old, would break and break.

I was sweating like a pig, after three or four hours of non-stop work. It started to rain. All in all, while I levered the rock Warren had managed to pull himself out about ten centimetres. Levering was made more difficult because the terrain behind Warren and the rock sloped up slightly. Furthest away from Warren 'his' rock had been broken by the fall. Why hadn't it in more places? Looking at the side of it answered my question. It was massive. From Warren's body its shape went down diagonally to a thickness of probably seventy-five centimetres at its thickest point. The sides were very black and rough. It made me shiver. The large flat top of it was the part that had come out of the mother rock and was surprisingly smooth. Patiently the erosion must have made its way down and cut it loose from the main rock. Waiting for Warren to pass!

Getting through the night

The rain meanwhile had grown to a full-on tropical shower. I had Warren draped in his warm sleeping bag, one that stays warm even when wet. Over this he wore his Gore-Tex raincoat which proved to be of priceless value. Every once in a while I felt so incredibly sad for him that I just sat next to him on the ground in the rain. My arm around his shoulder, massaging his massive upper body and talking calmly to him. Remembering a situation I was in once in the Pyrenees in France where I found great comfort when partner Peter comforted me in a similar fashion during a sno 3000 metres.

The calmness that Warren displayed will never stop to amaze me. The man never seemed to panic. Sometimes I was so tired that I had to leave him and I sat under the tarp. Desperately needing some time for myself and getting my thoughts reorganised. My legs would start to tremble and would not stop shaking until fifteen minutes had passed. I rolled a fag (thank God for tobacco) and tried to close my eyes for a few moments. Looking up again I saw Warren's silhouette in the dark background, his head a bit tilted to the right, rain smashing on his raincoat and I think it was then that I heard him moan. That sight brought back the adrenaline, pumping it through my veins and the tiredness disappeared momentarily while I went back up the mountain, trying to collect more wood.

There was no fear when I climbed up the green, forested walls of the small gorge we were in. I had neatly stored my socks and supporting soles next to my boots to dry them, but the water had washed them away. I was lucky to have held onto my boots. But I wore them without socks, and felt unstable. So while Warren sat in the dark in his complete helplessness I climbed, pocket knife at hand, torch in the mouth, shining through the wet green hell. Too much grass. Trees too thick. I climbed up the stem of a young eucalyptus and tried to bring it down by using my body weight. Hanging on the stem, somewhere above the creek, I hoped it would snap.

But it wouldn't snap. I could only break it into very tough and annoying strands. Its young green wood had too much life in it to allow it to be snapped. Of course! With the pocket knife I cut the strands. Soon my hands bled as I realised that by force the handles of the knife had come loose. It never hurt. I longed for tools — a small axe or something — but we had nothing on us.

When I returned to Warren he said that he had devised another way to get him out from underneath. He kept on thinking all night of ways to get himself out while I did the work. On his advice I collected rocks, different in size, length and weight, which I tried to get under the rock. I stood next to him, my back facing Warren's rock, and bent over with spread legs. In my hand I held a rock the size of a football and I used it to smash other rocks under the main one. Thereby hoping to lift it up. Warren would place the rocks with his left hand and I would try to bang them in place. Also a process of leverage.

'I like what I see. I like it,' Warren said encouragingly as the big rock seemed to lift slightly.

But I didn't like it. Indeed we had succeeded to move it a little but adding more rocks wouldn't improve our luck. It seemed there must be sand or a hole under it because I kept banging stones under the rock and it wouldn't move a millimetre.

It was another huge disappointment and it exposed my tiredness. The rock had not only pinned him down but it drained me of my reserves. There was no time to worry about that, however, and with another leverage attempt with wood we kept on trying to get it off. But again it didn't work. The water had risen frighteningly high by now. Warren was scared of getting drowned and when I looked up to follow the path of the creek upstream I saw that what had been a small water drop a few hundred metres away, and above us, had grown to a gigantic waterfall. I could see glimpses of its reflection during the night. All that water came our way with thundering force. I can still hear the noise sometimes in my sleep! It was terrifying.

A plane!

Some time during the night we heard a plane or maybe a helicopter way above us. The heavy rain had just stopped and Warren shouted that I should get a fire going.

'Grab a candle and hold it under some bark and twigs,' he yelled.

I went under the tarp, got my sketchbook and tore out a couple of sheets. In Warren's backpack I found a candle. Then I collected wood splints and old dry bits of bark and leaves and started to build a fire next to the tarpaulin on the spot where we had eaten many hours before. At first I couldn't get the moistened wood to burn but I kept on adding more paper and finally I got it going. By that time the plane or chopper had passed perhaps half an hour earlier.

A new shower in the ink black night finally took care of that problem when it extinguished the fire.

'Sorry, Warren. I can't get it working,' I said and he still had the strength to thank me for the effort, instead of showing his disappointment.

I sat next to him again and we tried to figure out another way in which I could get him out. We didn't say much to each other. Each of us was aware of the race against time and the elements. Time was already running out. All our exploits in releasing him were to no avail. I had to protect my strength and by doing so I could have the chance to save Warren when morning came. I kept working against the odds to curb my thoughts and sense of total desperation.

More tree branches had to be taken down. I needed more wood! Up I went again, crawling through the bush, torch in the mouth, and I managed to get some stems down with which I once again tried to lever. Sometimes I would actually get some leverage and, almost happy, both Warren and I reacted with great enthusiasm. It was possible to stick wood under the sharp point that was near his right knee, sticking it under the rock, parallel with his leg and ending on the ground near his foot. A few metres behind him I'd jump and sit with my body weight on the branch. While I worked the branch Warren would use all his strength to pull himself out, his hands on the edge of the rock in front of him and with a determined look on his face. Literally peeling off the skin of his legs!

The long night

The night advanced extremely slowly. After five hours of near useless, energy-draining work I needed a serious rest. I crawled into the sleeping bag, lay down and closed my eyes, occasionally yelling out into the darkness to see if he was all right.

'How ya going Warren? Are you all right?'

'Yeah, mate. Yes,' he would reply and I would close my eyes again to get some rest. Never for long, however. *Are you all right?* What a stupid thing to ask! Realising that he was fighting for his life, soon I would be back with him.

Around 4.00am I realised I should prepare Warren and myself for the descent. We launched one final attempt to get him loose, mentally collecting and organising our willpower and strength. But I had to give up rather early as I was completely exhausted. 'The only way for him to stay alive,' I thought, 'is to get a rescue party up.'

I knew what I had to do and once again sat next to Warren and discussed my plan. Firstly I made a small wall of stones to his right, to function as a kind of dam if the water kept on rising. Behind his back I made some sort of chair. All the broken pieces of wood at least had a function. So I made a chair and stuck his Therm-a-rest between his back and the pile of wood. That way he had more comfort and could allow himself to relax his back and shoulders during the long day and night that was ahead of him.

The rain had stopped at about 3.00am and the water level was dropping quickly now, as mountain streams always do. By 5.00am some sort of new life or spirit had come into me and I was under the tarp once more, starting preparations for the most important task in my life. In retrospect I think this energy had something to do with being able to be useful — wrapping up Warren's necessities and concentrating on getting down in one piece. After all, it was one disappointment after another trying to get him free.

I found three plastic shopping bags in Warren's pack and filled one up with food: muesli, dried fruits, an apple, avocado, bread and cheese, crackers and a few muesli bars. In the other bag I put some clothes: an extra shirt and a grey body warmer, a few pairs of socks which he could wear as gloves, a scarf which he could use as a bandanna and a cap for if it got hot again during the day. The third bag contained his diary and pen, insect repellent and his torch. His toothpaste and brush would keep him a little occupied also. A cord which I removed from the tarp, I put through the bag handles and hung it around his neck. The bags were positioned in front of him on the rock, which by now functioned as a table. That way he couldn't lose them. Another flash flood could really make things even more serious up there. He drank from a green mug, simply by scooping it into the water around him.

Earlier, before the rains came in seriously, I had wrapped his right foot in a plastic bag. The water had washed away the bag and later, when I examined his foot, I saw that all colour had left the flesh. It looked very bad.

Then I went back under the tarp and started to pack my own necessities. Many items had been washed away by the water and I missed my supporting soles — very important for steady feet on my hike down. Later I realised I had lost my water bottle and sunhat, as well as my socks, but these items were easily replaced. In this madness I didn't need them. I put on some of Warren's socks. When I had packed my stuff I went back out and sat next to him. I told him I was wearing his socks and why. This was one time when I felt like crying but I couldn't allow myself to get emotional. Not here! Warren's attitude was so impressive that we fed off each other emotionally. Because he stayed calm, I stayed calm, and vice versa.

First light

Slowly the first light of April 10th appeared. I had decided to leave as soon as that moment would arise but had to wait longer as it could get me into trouble. The mist and grey atmosphere scared me. At 6.30am I repeated to Warren that the only way to get him out of there was to make it down in one piece and find help. He would have to prepare himself mentally for at least another day and night before he possibly could be rescued.

We were hoping that there might be fishing boats in Little Ramsay Bay, as there were when we went up. I told him to keep writing in his diary and to try to meditate. I had just read a lot about the use of meditation, and I thought it might help him not to pass out or 'lose it'.

'Don't give up Warren. Stay positive.'

I worried that he would lose consciousness. I looked at his lean face and noticed an incredible fear in his expression. His eyes sat deep in his forehead now. A bald, pale face with frightened eyes, almost as black as coal.

'I rely on you, mate. Think about every step you make,' he said and I replied that I was going to get him out of the park.

'Tomorrow night, you're out of here.'

To which he answered, 'You're sounding pretty confident, mate.' I told him I *was* confident and knew for certain that I was going to get him out — that he, like me, must have read stories about people who came through even worse circumstances.

'You are very tough and have to hang in there. Besides I want to see your ugly face when you're back down in the world,' I joked to him.

Using this kind of talk we tried to ease our fears a little. Still, it wasn't time to leave yet. I sat next to him and both of us didn't speak for a few minutes. Before I could cross the physical boundary that was waiting for me I had to cross the mental threshold. Because leaving somebody behind in a helpless position and approaching the dangers of the descent were not a piece of cake. I was aware of that but had to get out. The reality of that made it easier for me. Also that I could undertake action that I held in my own hands was positive. Nothing was going to stop me before I reached the beach!

'Go well!'

I kissed Warren on the forehead, got up and swung my pack over my shoulders. It was heavier than yesterday, with a soaking wet sleeping bag inside it. I looked down to where I had to go and for a moment felt scared. More daylight had come to our position and I realised I was looking down into a wild and angry waterfall, held in place by dense bush. Grey and green. There was no route to make out in this landscape any more. Just water, wet slippery boulders and rainforest. Somehow I should get down there. Down to the beach.

I shook hands with Warren and started my first nervous steps. I remember that I slipped immediately and heard Warren yell, 'Go bush, mate. GO BUSH.'

My slip must have scared the early daylights out of him. His survival depended on my safe descent. I said I would, and then Warren spoke the last words, which were, 'Go well! Go well!'

THE ULTIMATE TEST

In the moments following Geert's departure, I began to confront what I now had to face, what I hadn't even wanted to think about while there was still some chance of avoiding it.

This is it mate, this is your ultimate test. This is the one you've been preparing yourself for all your life. I hope you've got your shit together. You better be good enough, coz it's all up to you now mate.

Why did you come here? Why put yourself so far away from civilisation? Is this what you wanted? Is this a tough enough test for you?

Should I even be here? Am I strong enough to be so far from civilisation like this?

The questions surged through my head, threatening to crush me.

After one of my first bushwalks, Mum expressed her concern for my safety. 'If I die out there, Mum, it means I wasn't good enough,' came my reply, much to her horror. 'I'd rather die out there, than under some dickhead's car in a supermarket car park!'

But now, faced with the harsh reality of it, was it true? *Am I ready to die like this, out here, completely and utterly alone?*

Hot tears rolled down my face to give me my answer. *Not yet, I'm not. No, I can't die like this.*

This feeling of centrality, of feeling that you are the one; that your whole universe revolves around one person; that it doesn't matter what goes on around you, you are at the helm of your own destiny — it had first come to me six or seven years before, in the US. Of course, the circumstances weren't quite the same, but I remember it clearly.

Dirty had just stepped on a bus in LA, bound for the airport. He was flying home, just as Dig and Pete had done a few weeks before, and Dave a month before them. That left me. The five of us had arrived together three months earlier and we'd basically partied our way around the States. Everyone else had taken time off work for the trip. I hadn't. I had thrown in my career as a technical officer because I figured there had to be more to life than shuffling pieces of paper around that nobody took any notice of. It was the first time I'd thrown my cards into the air. Standing at the bus stop now, watching the bus drive away with the only person I knew within 20,000 kilometres on board, I had an overwhelming sense of excitement. This was it. This was what

I'd left home indefinitely for. The last three months had been fun, but my real journey had only just begun.

And I felt much the same way now. Even though I knew my life was in Geert's hands, he had to make it out; I had no control over any aspect of that. I couldn't make him go any faster. On the contrary, I wanted him to take it carefully, to be sure he made it. But still, I knew that my goal was just to hang in there. To make sure I was still alive when the rescue crew arrived. The thought that I might not be good enough to do it terrified me.

The rain had stopped now, the sun spreading warmly over my gully early, heralding the beginning of another hot day. I felt like a wounded animal, like those you see in African documentaries, just sitting there waiting to be discovered and finished off. I managed to eat a few pieces of dried paw-paw; I was going to need some energy. The water level, still around my waist, was sapping the heat from my body. I was constantly having to adjust the sleeping bag to counter cold spots. Knowing I was going to have to wait at least until the next morning was agonising. The very thought that, no matter what, I was stuck there for another 24 hours at least, hung like a lead weight around my neck. Unable to accept my fate, I felt so utterly useless just lying there.

What do you think you're doing just lying there? You've got to get out!

Picking up my stone wedge again, I placed it in the gap between the top of the pile of stones and the ceiling of the overhang, holding it with my left hand, then belting it as hard as possible with the hammer stone in my right. And again and again. I kept going until exhausted.

C'mon you weak bastard! What the hell are you doing? Nobody else is going to get you out of here. What if Geert doesn't make it back? Then what are you gonna do?

At that I'd start again, working frantically before falling back in a heap yet again. Lying back, feeling like a total failure, my mind would then take the other side.

Hell! What are you doing? Jesus mate, take it easy! You've got to save your energy! Keep that up and you haven't got a chance!

I rode that roller coaster all day. Busting my gut, then cursing myself for being so stupid. Finally, I accepted the inevitable. I wasn't going anywhere.

SEEING THE LIGHT

Breathing hard, bent over with both hands on my trembling knees, looking down at feet that I could barely move, I'd have to say that I'd rather have been elsewhere. I'd never felt so exhausted, so totally drained of energy. I felt like the other toy in the Energizer commercials, the one whose inferior batteries cark it prematurely, leaving the Energizer equipped guy to power on. *That's who I am. The guy who can't hack it.*

'Just leave me here, I'll go back down to the bus.'

All I wanted to do was go home. At one point, I dropped to the ground as my legs gave way underneath me, my calf trying to turn itself inside out. A feeling of utter uselessness filled me. *I can't do this. It's too hard!*

But of course going home was out of the question. This was a team effort, a team building, character building exercise. I was 19 years old, in the third year of my four-year apprenticeship as a ranger/farmer with the Gas & Fuel Corporation of Victoria. Based in Ballarat, just over an hour west of Melbourne, my job was to carry out maintenance on the 120-kilometre gas pipeline between the two cities. Somebody had figured that, in order to communicate with the farmers whose land our high-pressure pipeline passed through, we needed to do a four-year farming apprenticeship! Over the first three years, I spent one week of each month attending trade school at the Wangaratta College of TAFE in northern Victoria.

Now, don't get me wrong. I learnt some handy skills over those four years. How to de-horn cattle, for instance; how to knock up a quick mallee gate. What to do when the sheep are all flyblown, and the Massey Ferguson just *will not* turn over. Chris Truscott, who held the same position on the Gippsland pipeline, and I were the two representatives of the Gas & Fuel. Our classmates were all sons of local farmers who'd sent their boys off to TAFE to get some kind of qualification behind them before they took over the family farm. Finding it difficult to see any relevance between our jobs and shearing sheep, we were both fairly disillusioned with the whole situation. When I learned we would be going on a four-day walk up into the Bogong high plains, I looked at it as a kind of holiday away from the more mundane aspects of the course.

John Kirby, who had organised this part of the course, was not your average teacher (as I began to appreciate more as I got older). I didn't realise it at the time, but he was really trying to instil in us an understanding of the land, not just for farming purposes, but to recognise our place in it. Above all, our responsibility to it as farmers who rely on the land for a living. I'm sure he must have gone to great lengths to have this trip included as part of the curriculum, as it would have been seen by some of his peers (as it was to me) to be completely irrelevant.

John suggested, a month before our hiking trip, that it would be a good idea if we spent some time working on fitness, as this would be a demanding walk.

Yeah right! How hard can it be? We're only walking; it's not as if we'll be running up there!

I went for a couple of easy four to five kilometre runs over the next month, nothing over the top. I was nineteen for Christ's sake! All I wanted to do when I wasn't working was drink beer and have a good time!

'It would be better if you could find some decent hills to train on,' had been John's final suggestion as we left that Friday afternoon. *Yeah, no problem!*

On the Tuesday afternoon one of the other teachers dropped us off at the trail head campsite at Mountain Creek, where we made camp for the night. We were all still treating the whole adventure as a bit of a joke, having no idea whatsoever what could possibly lie ahead. I crawled out of the tent next morning into the high country mist wearing all the clothing I'd brought with me, including the woollen army pants. After a hurried breakfast, we were off, at a leisurely pace, along a dirt forestry track.

This isn't so bad. What was all the fuss about having to be fit? For this!

We'd split into our own little groups, just cruising along talking trash, when John called out from behind, 'OK, turn right where you are now!' I looked right to see a small track disappearing into the trees, but my attention was drawn skyward as I tilted my head back to find the horizon.

'Shit!' was all I could say as my eyes followed the zigzag track snaking its way up the steep northern slope of Mount Bogong. Over the course of the next four or five hours, I came to appreciate why it was called 'The Staircase'.

My body almost begged me to stop every step of the way, the straps on my pack digging into my soft shoulders. Heart pounding, I'd stop every two to three minutes to lean forward with my hands on my knees, gulping in huge lungfuls of air. I wanted to just take my pack off and lie down, dead, but John wouldn't have a bar of it.

'C'mon, we can't stop here. We've still got a lot of ground to cover. You'll find it much easier if you keep moving. We'll stop for a break up at the hut.'

Bloody hell! What am I doing here? What does this have to do with anything?

I felt so weak, yet I took my anger out on John, blaming him for my predicament. I started to hate him, cursing him for somehow getting us into this as part of our course. 'I bet he's getting a real kick out of this,' I thought, as he'd shown a dislike for Chris and myself due to our lack of interest in parts of the curriculum.

I wasn't the only one doing it hard. A couple of us actually wanted to go back.

'Nobody's going back! We're all in this together. There's no one back at the campsite. They're not picking us up till Friday at Falls Creek. It's as simple as that.'

When it seemed like I couldn't possibly go any further, I raised my head from my sunken shoulders to see, not just a very steep hill in front of me, but a looming horizon. Somehow, we had reached the top. I was in too much pain, both physical and emotional, to gain any appreciation of the view at all. All I could do was savour the fact that we weren't actually walking!

I had a quick glance around at the land lying far below, but before I'd had a chance to get my breath back, we were off again. My feet screamed inside a pair of inadequate desert boots. I'd thought they'd be OK for the trip, but I was now finding out the hard way that they were far from up to scratch. The walking became more bearable now that the main climb lay behind us, but I still literally staggered into Cleve Cole hut that afternoon.

Stepping gingerly around the camp, I felt ashamed of my weakness earlier and avoided any conversation about the day's events. I felt like an outsider, that the others were now worried that I might hold up the trip and we'd still be walking into the weekend. Everybody had complained during the course of the day, but I didn't think they were doing it as hard as I was. I really felt like I was letting the side down and was so angry with myself for being unfit, so piss-weak.

The next day's walking, though not as steep, was not much easier. The second day's walking on any trip, as I later learned, is usually harder than the first because you've got the 'whole-body-aching' syndrome from the abuse your body has copped the day before. I still felt like I'd been hit by a truck at the end of the second day, but at least I hadn't complained to the point of wanting to go home!

That night, instead of setting up camp as we had previously, John had something else in mind. Each of us was sent in a different direction from camp, at least a couple of hundred metres away, with a box of matches, some flour, a water bottle and the warmest clothes we had.

'Now, I don't want to see you guys again until morning. Make sure you follow your bearings if you leave your camp to get water, which I suggest you do. And don't cop out and go and visit someone else's camp. This is just for one night. I'm sure you'll be able to handle it.'

As I lay next to the fire alone that night I felt my strength begin to grow. I may not have been fit enough for the actual walking, but now I was relying on a skill that would serve me well into the future: the skill of just keeping my shit together, of not panicking, when removed from the structured routine of everyday life. I knew that all I had to do was collect enough firewood to keep me going for the night and I'd be OK. I cooked up plenty of damper through the night, falling asleep with a full stomach, only to be woken by the dying fire. Feeding it back into life, I gazed up at the stars and for the first time imagined myself floating upwards, trying to gain a perspective of my little camp on this mountain, what it must look like from above. Then, from further away, zooming up to see where this mountain fits into things in relation to the city far away. And where that city fits in, trying to comprehend my place on the earth itself. *Try it. It'll freak you out!*

It felt so liberating to be outside, under a blanket of stars instead of cocooned safely inside a concrete suburban box. Vulnerable and exposed, I felt so much stronger for being able to do it. *I don't need that roof over my head to feel safe and secure.* I felt safe and secure within myself and it made my skin crawl with excitement. Filled with a sense of wonder of the total reality of it all, I felt at peace with the world for the first time in my life.

I learned a lot about myself that night. I realised that I wasn't really that weak. Unfit, yes; but I could change that (and I did, as soon as I got back, joining a gym and starting a fitness program, looking after myself a bit more than I had been). I'd begun the expansion of my comfort zone.

It was with great satisfaction that I walked back into camp that morning. Some of the other guys hadn't lasted the night alone, returning to their tents before dawn. I couldn't understand why they could not go through with it. Was it because they couldn't stand their own company? Could they have been so afraid that they had to return to the safety of John's camp?

Of course, male bravado prevented any real reasons being offered; rather, what was put forward was 'My fire kept going out', or 'I ran out of water'. I couldn't help wondering what they would have done if they had been in the same situation without the escape hatch. Lain down and died? I felt a hell of a lot better about myself now, and about my part in the team — like I had proven myself. I began to appreciate the rest of the trip from that point on. Some parts of the walk got harder, but I used the knowledge gained during the night — that I could do anything — to push myself on. I even started to enjoy it. At one point, high on a ridge, I looked back in amazement as John pointed out where we'd come from that morning. It was so far away, I could scarcely believe him.

I walked out of the bush two days later very sore and extremely tired, but with such a sense of achievement. We'd covered about 40 kilometres over three days, into a place where relatively few people had been. It wasn't until 12 months later, when I had the urge to do it all again, that I realised those few days had set me on a new course. A course with a number of streams, one of which I'm still travelling today. That events like that happen for a reason, and you can either ignore them and go about life as usual; or you can seize them, allowing them to transport you into new realms.

INTO THE BLACK

In between bouts of restlessness, reaching into one of the bags for some paw-paw spears, I caught a glimpse of my diary. I'd meant to pick it up a few times before but couldn't do it. To start writing would mean I'd accepted defeat.

I'm getting out of here, I don't really need to write anything, do I?

I knew why Geert had put my diary in the bag. I hadn't asked him to and it was something we couldn't have talked about. He would have wanted it with him if he was in my position and, though *I* hadn't thought of it, I was glad *he* had.

I started writing, explaining what had happened; but I quickly felt a strong sense of finality and had to stop. I felt like I'd be tempting fate by writing in the past tense and that didn't help me to stay positive. I put the diary away and slumped forward over the slab again. Trying to numb my mind, to take away the pain that kept threatening to engulf me completely. All I could think about was Geert, and how he was coping with his descent.

Please, Geert. You've got to get down.

My hearing must have become so intensified that the sound of aircraft constantly had me reaching for the blue poly tarp. It acted both as my protection (from the rain and the intense North Queensland sun that seemed hell bent on frying me), and as a signal to any aircraft that may happen to fly overhead. I'd reach for it at the slightest hum in the distance, stretching it out above my head when I thought an aircraft was close enough possibly to notice me. Of course, I never *saw* one, but that didn't stop me pulling it out every time. *Please! Somebody fly over this way!* I was desperate for a plane to see me, for them to raise the alarm so I wouldn't have to wait until Geert made it out.

'Christ, he wouldn't even be halfway down yet!' I thought.

Lying back, utterly dejected, I contemplated my fate. *What's it going to be like to die? Will I die today? Is this how I'm going to die? Is it going to be painful? Can it possibly hurt any more than this or do you actually have to be in more pain before you die?*

I'd never been this close to dying before, so how was I supposed to know what it feels like? Sure, like everyone else, I would lie in bed some nights and start to think about the whole concept of life. Then, it would just get too much. I'd shudder at the intensity, my head shaking involuntarily at the incomprehensible concept of ceasing to exist, trying to dislodge the very thought from my mind. *What the hell are we doing here anyway? How can it all just finish? Will I still be conscious, actually existing on another plane? I'd like to think so, but I doubt it. And yet, how can it possibly be otherwise …?*

Did I even achieve anything while I existed or was mine just another wasted life? Is there any such thing as a wasted life? Or is every life intrinsically important? Sounds like wishful thinking to me. Haven't we as humans just elevated ourselves to such a high state of importance, put ourselves above all other beings? Is there any merit in that? Aren't we all just animals, the same as the birds and the bees?

Sometimes I think I'm contradicting myself, with the concept of us all being animals, set against the terrifying impossibility of coming to an end.

My mind drifted back to another time and place, far, far away, where I'd had my first close encounter with my own mortality.

ZAIRE

June 1992 saw my arrival in Africa. After living in London and travelling throughout Europe for the previous two years, I'd yearned for some real adventure. Europe just didn't interest me any more. Sure, I'd had a good time there — probably too good. I'd hitched my way across Germany numerous times, once right through to Turkey's north-east coast. I'd been at Berlin's Brandenburg Gate at midnight on the night of Germany's reunification, witnessing east and west become one. I'd slept on the beach at Gallipoli; haunted by the tragedy that took place on the sand on which I lay. I'd travelled around Ireland on a diet of soda bread and Guinness, sitting in ancient pubs as old men sang heart-rending songs of love and war.

But Africa had drawn me to her, like a moth to the flame. I wanted to see how the world used to be. Wanted to experience it, be moulded by it.

From the moment I arrived, stepping out of the terminal at Nairobi airport, I sensed a difference in the very air. Africa has a timelessness about it that is very difficult to explain. I almost felt as if I had arrived home. A home I had never known. Perhaps I had only ever visited in my dreams. After spending the first month in Kenya and Tanzania, drifting from the savanna plains of the Serengeti to the island paradise of Kiwayu, it was time to get down to business.

My plan was to travel south through Zaire along the Congo River. I had heard that Zaire was a wild country, with danger and adventure lurking around every corner; that it was untamed and untameable. This was the Africa I wanted to see, not the colonial remnants left behind by the Europeans. I would be travelling on my own, preferring it that way due to the relative instability of the country. I didn't want to be responsible for anyone else if Zaire was to be as wild as rumour had it. Besides, the challenge of travelling alone in such a wild place was one of the main reasons for coming to Africa.

Plans, being what they are, don't always run smoothly. I had picked up a couple of nasty stomach bugs while hiking in the Ruwenzori Mountains, the fabled, mist shrouded range straddling the Ugandan–Zairean border. In a moment of carelessness, I assumed that the water gathering in small pools behind Elena Hut would be safe. Perched precariously at 4540 metres, Elena Hut sits just below the glacier crowning Margherita Peak, Mount Stanley. Being the tallest mountain in the Ruwenzori range, and hence not receiving a hell of a lot of visitors, you could be forgiven for assuming the water to be clean. Couldn't you?

With a combination of amoebic dysentery and giardia, I decided against throwing myself straight into the perils of Zaire. It made much more sense to rest awhile in Uganda, slowly making my way towards its south-western border with Rwanda, my goal being to reach the Virunga Park Du Nationale, just across the border. The park is the last remaining habitat of the mountain gorilla, and I wanted to see them in the wild, in their own environment, before they came to exist only in zoos. On arrival in Kisoro, the last Ugandan town before the border, I learned that the civil war had again flared in Rwanda, and the border had been closed. A couple of Kiwis, Jim and Clare, assured me the border on the other side of the country, shared with Tanzania, was still open, so I decided to join them in a mad trip that took us three days to get to a place less than 50 kilometres as the crow flies from our point of origin.

At one stage I travelled in the back of a closed container,

three-quarters full with bananas, while Jim and Clare rode in the front with the driver. Sharing the space with two of the plantation workers, I bounced between the bananas and the container ceiling as we careered down the pot-holed, poor excuse for a road! Two hours later the smiling driver dropped us off to continue in another direction, leaving us waving goodbye at a dusty intersection in the middle of nowhere, me covered in mashed banana!

It wasn't long before the next ride appeared. This time I got to ride in the cabin — along with six others! Crammed in like sardines, we made our way through the mountainous Rwandan countryside, our toothless driver grinning in embarrassment when reaching for low gear as Claire, straddling the gearstick, moaned her appreciation! It was good for a laugh until he slowed to pick up another two blokes hitching on the roadside. *Where on earth is he going to put them?*

Jim and I volunteered to ride shotgun standing on the truck's wheel arches. Raised a few eyebrows, it did, a couple of *mzungus* (whites) riding like that. We must have got a few laughs.

Seeing the mountain gorillas of the Virungas would have to be one of the most magical experiences of my life. I was a visitor in their realm, an intruder, but at the same time I was aware that we are responsible for the future of these great forest dwellers, totally in tune with their environment. Yet here we are, totally dependent on the equipment we've brought with us, visitors in every sense of the word; and their future depends on us, mankind. Their survival depends on our finding a solution to the ever-increasing needs of the local farmers who believe it is their only option to push their cultivated land up the side of the hill, reducing the gorillas' domain.

It took us two full hours to find them, our guides hacking a path through the almost impenetrable jungle with machetes. Once their initial apprehension at our intrusion subsided, they went about their merry way, accepting our presence to the point of ignoring us. The wisdom in the eye of the silverback brought a lump to my throat, his pride and his very presence overwhelming. I held so much respect for him, but at the same time so much pity.

How could such majestic beings' future be held in the hands of humans who'd long ago lost their connection to the land? Did their demise begin when fat, rich bastards around the world decided a gorilla's hand would look cool as an ashtray in their office? Or did it begin before that, back when the Lord told us that the animals were there for us to use?

After a few days' rest in Kigali, Rwanda's capital, I began to feel strong again and decided I was ready to begin my journey into Zaire. My mission was to make my way overland east of Lake Kivu, from Bukavu to the Zaire River, formerly the Congo. From there, I would travel downstream on the legendary floating village that plied the great river, taking two to three weeks to reach Lubambashi. It wasn't a trip to be taken lightly and I agonised over the decision of whether to go or not. Believing my health was on the mend, I crossed the border into Zaire, walking the four or five kilometres of no-man's land between Gisenyi (Rwanda) and Goma (Zaire). No sooner had I crossed the border than I was struck down again, being forced to rest for another few days.

Finally, after a horrendous ferry trip the length of the magnificent Lake Kivu, I reached Bukavu. This would be my last taste of relative civilisation before heading into the dark heart of Africa, so I spent a few days just relaxing while investigating transport inland.

It took me a couple of days to find someone willing to take me to Kindu, a village 250 kilometres west, on the banks of the mighty Congo. Most people tried to talk me out of the journey altogether, shaking their heads in concern, saying 'Bad, very bad. Road, no good' in broken Swahili. I'd discovered quite early on my arrival in Zaire that my limited Swahili would be all but useless. Zaire is a French speaking country, and is too far away from the slave-trading east coast, where the language developed, for Swahili to be widely spoken. Some people have a limited knowledge of it, but they are few and far between. Most people in the east speak Lingala, a language I'm having trouble picking up. My refusal to learn any French out of principle was now beginning to suffer some drawbacks.

I finally made arrangements to get on a truck leaving at 7.00am the following morning, agreed on a price with the driver, then took to the market to pick up supplies. With trepidation I lay in bed that night hoping everything would fall into place. That I had the departure time right, that he was leaving from the same place we spoke at yesterday. Things like that are easy to stuff up when making a plan without a common language. But there was to be no problem with minor details like that. What he'd failed to tell me were two fairly important bits of information of a much more serious nature!

The first was that the road was passable to vehicles only for the first 150 kilometres. The rest must be travelled on foot. That normally wouldn't be a problem, but in the state I was in, I had trouble walking a single kilometre!

The second vital piece of missing information was that the whole area I would be travelling through was a declared mineral zone, being full of gold and precious gems — so precious that everybody passing through would need a special permit. Of course, I wouldn't know this until the military police knocked on my door at 7.00am after arriving late the night before.

I turned up at the agreed spot at 6.00am the following morning, to be greeted by the scene of confusion that is mandatory on any African journey. From there, the saga went as follows.

The truck is surrounded with shouting and wildly gesticulating people, all trying to climb onto the vehicle as if it's a lifeboat in shark infested waters. At the same time, the crew are trying to load the cargo, which includes about twenty-five twenty-litre plastic drums. They're tied on the back, creating a bizarre, wedding vehicle effect!

An hour later, I'm still trying to get my legs through the entanglement of everybody else's, the truck lurches forward and we're off — thirty of us, jammed on top of an open truck, on top of the cargo; my white face standing out starkly in a sea of black. I soon learn that I'm the only English speaker on board, apart from Joseph, a school teacher on his way home to Kindu. Nobody else pays me much notice; in fact, they seem to resent me being there. Hoping like hell that my stomach and bowels will stay under control, I settle uncomfortably into the nest of limbs.

That day we cover about 100 kilometres on fairly decent roads — by Zairean standards, anyway — passing through spectacular country of huge valleys set in lush tropical rainforest. Huge rivers, with gangs of men working siftings on the banks, flow through the valleys below. The rivers have been diverted in places, by hand, by men searching for riches.

The truck has a crew of four young guys whose sole purpose is to keep the show on the road. They don't do much for the first few hours, and I wonder why all four of them are on board. Apart from loading the additional supplies we pick up on the way, their main pastime is to outdo each other in hanging shit on me! They're tough bastards; you'd want to be, doing their jobs. One guy's wearing a lone shoe. He's constantly eyeing my hiking boots. It's become cool, apparently, to give me a hard time on my every move. I can't understand a word they're saying but it's pretty obvious. Whenever we all have to climb back into the truck after loading more supplies, which is often, they're all laughing at me climbing the side of the truck in my piss-weak state. I quickly begin to hate their guts.

Night falls and it's obvious that we ain't stopping. The stars remain hidden behind a cloak of black cloud, and it's not long after the first forks of lightning that the rain begins to fall. As we drive deeper into the forest, the road becomes increasingly overgrown, the passing of trucks like ours the only thing stopping the road from being completely grown over. When the first branch swoops at us, I laugh along with everybody else (after my initial surprise). When the branches start to increase in size, I start to get a bit concerned (along with everybody else!). The yell of what I quickly presume to be Lingala for 'duck!' becomes more and more prevalent, until we're all ducking under huge sweeping branches every few seconds. At first I sit up with the thrill seekers, eyes wide for the next branch to duck under. As they keep coming thicker and faster, I'm spending less and less time sitting up. Because I'm facing backwards, I'm having to look over my shoulder to see what's coming. As I lift my head, I'm struck a blow so hard that at first I'm not even sure whether my head's still on my shoulders.

Once my head finally stops spinning, I am certain I have broken my neck. One of those young shitheads laughs! Hating him even more doesn't help. I stay hunched for the next couple of hours, my face pressed against my knees, not daring to look up. We finally reach a small village around midnight, and all clamber out before heading off in different directions in search of food and shelter. After a quick meal, I find myself a place to stay for the night. As I lie in bed in a mud hut-cum-hotel, I can't help but wonder what the hell I'm doing here. *Mate, you're not strong enough to be doing this! You could die here and no one would ever know. Do you really need to be doing this? What the hell are you trying to prove?*

It's still dark when I'm woken by the driver, and he's not happy. It seems we had our wires crossed last night when, I thought, he'd agreed to wake me in the morning. Well, he did wake me, I suppose. About two minutes before we were ready to leave! Everyone else is already on the truck and ready to go while I'm frantically throwing my gear into my pack. I run over and heave my pack up over the side, climbing up to be greeted with a tirade of abuse. Great, the sun is hardly even up, and these guys are giving me hell already. I imagine what they're saying; *What's wrong with you? You're holding us all up, you useless mzungu! Get your shit together!*

I'm completely pissed off, and losing it quickly. I give them shit back in English, knowing they can't understand a word I'm saying, but also aware that they'll get the message the same as I am. I feel like the school dickhead, the one that everybody picks on just because he deserves it. I didn't think things could possibly get any worse than last night's hell trip, but they have indeed taken a turn for the worse within minutes of departing!

The state of the road is deteriorating (I wouldn't imagine that possible if I hadn't seen and felt it for myself), resembling a motor-cross track more than a road. It is nothing more than a quagmire in places, with mud-pits more than a metre deep stretching for thirty or forty metres at times. We come upon the first one within minutes of clearing town, and immediately become bogged in it. Everybody gets out and the guys go to work with shovels, spending the next hour digging us out. After a couple of failed attempts, they begin unloading the whole truck to give us more hope of getting out. The rest of us begin walking the first of many kilometres. Half an hour later, a couple of kilometres down the track, the truck catches up to us, engine roaring as the driver maintains his speed to keep the truck moving. He guns it straight past us and, after feeling a little apprehensive at first, I realise there's no need to be alarmed. With the state of the road, I won't be surprised if we all walk the whole way to Kindu!

When we finally do get back in the truck, I quickly wish we hadn't.

The road cut into the side of a very steeply sloping mountain, hundreds of metres above the river below. Needing to keep our speed up to avoid being continuously bogged, the truck lurches from side to side as one side, then the other, sinks into the deep wheel ruts. The deeper ruts see us drop suddenly to one side, at times balancing precariously, before dropping down onto four wheels again. My stomach drops as I look over the side into the ravine below.

This is it. It's all over!

If the truck leaves the road here, there's no doubt we'll all die. Sitting atop the truck, with my legs entwined with theirs, I'll never be able to break free and jump if we do start to roll. But how far would the truck have to roll before I'd consider jumping? I realise I would have jumped a dozen times already if I could have — that's how certain I am that we're going to roll.

Sometimes we tip the other way, towards the embankment, slamming hard into the earthen wall, then scraping along it before being thrown across towards the edge once more.

I have never been so terrified, almost crying out in panic. I am so certain I'll die. I think of all the people I'll never see again. Whether my family will ever even hear of my fate, instead having to suffer the uncertainty of having me listed as missing, somewhere in Zaire. It happens in Zaire. If you're lucky, someone may hand your passport over to the relevant authorities and inform them of what happened. But only if you're lucky.

What the hell are you doing this for? It's not fair on everybody else, especially Mum. What are you trying to prove?

I feel selfish for what I am doing for the first time in my life. Joseph offers me some comfort when I ask him anxiously whether any trucks have actually gone over the side. 'Many,' he replies. 'But only if God wishes it to be.'

Not being the religious type, I find no comfort in his assurance at all, and continue the journey certain I will die at any moment, holding on in white-knuckled terror each time the truck lurches over towards the edge, my life in the balance.

THIRSTY

Leaning back into my Therm-a-rest, taking in everything around me — the rugged peaks, the whistling birds, the gentle breeze — I realised that, if this was to be my final resting place, I couldn't have picked a better one.

This is the way I've always said I'd like to go. But is it? Totally alone? Haven't I already spent too much of my life alone? Do I have to die alone as well?

I thought about all the people I loved, especially those I'd wished I could have loved more. Of how I wished I'd told them how I really felt before now, before it was too late. I went through all my regrets, but at the end of the day decided that I'd actually done a fair bit in my life. It was really only in love that I felt my life had been unfulfilled; it was the one thing missing. Sometimes I wondered whether it existed at all.

I was so thirsty. So very thirsty. It seemed that I couldn't possibly drink enough, reaching beside me to fill my cup continuously. 'Well, there's no shortage of water,' I thought, though the level had steadied right out. The fear of drowning had ebbed away with the water that threatened me. The flow of water cascading over the buttress upstream had quelled now. It was still coming over all right, but nothing like it had been until mid-morning.

That granite face was also blocking my view of our intended destination, the summit of Mount Bowen. I had a pretty good view of 'the thumb' from where I sat, though — an impressive peak in itself, jutting high, as the name suggests, like a giant thumbs up. Could it be the island's way of telling me 'You'll be right mate'? or was it more along the lines of 'We've got you now mate, now you're finished'?

I began to feel in one way that I was now totally a 'part of nature' — that, being trapped like this, I was at her mercy, subject to all her realities, realities we escape by existing in our little protective bubbles.

I'm constantly thinking about Geert and how he is going on his journey downstream.

Could he have possibly made good enough time to have flagged down a boat at Little Ramsay Bay already? Is it possible that they could be on their way to get me out right now?

I had the nightmarish vision of Geert lying injured somewhere downstream.

No, he's gonna make it. He's got to.

The day seemed to go on forever, time running in some kind of perverse slow motion. I longed for the night, just to get it over with.

The quicker it got dark, the quicker it would get light again. I knew also that it would be much easier to be seen at night time, my trusty sabre-light torch held under the blue poly tarp becoming a highly visible beacon from the air. In some ways it would actually make a better signal than a fire, which could be interpreted as just another campfire. But a flashing blue beacon would have to pose some kind of question to the beholder. Therefore, I'd reach for the torch whenever I heard a sound, which was often. But I could not get used to my disappointment each time the hum of a distant engine failed to come closer and just veered off in another direction.

God, I'm cold. So cold.

Rubbing my hands on both arms, trying to keep them warm. Constantly rearranging the sleeping bag around my waist, the cold spots becoming too much as the water flowed straight through it. The current dragging it off me, letting the water swirl around my unprotected body, sapping my heat and energy away. Colder and colder I grew, thoughts of hypothermia filling my head. I became increasingly afraid to go to sleep. 'Go to sleep now and you won't wake up' was the warning echoing through my mind. But it came to me in short stints, at times leaving me in such a surreal state that I had trouble afterwards determining whether I had been awake or asleep.

GEERT VAN KEULEN: **Descent**

The descent was ten times worse than the climb! An amazing amount of water was coming down and there wasn't much of the area that I was able to recognise. It all looked the same. After a few steps I lost visual contact with Warren and the noise of the water destroyed any chance to communicate verbally. Not satisfied with that, I yelled out one final time, 'See you Warren.' I don't think he could have heard me.

I made it down the first slippery boulder. Thousands more to come! The fear disappeared once more and was replaced by yet another burst of adrenaline. Slowly, very unsteady at first, I started to go down. My pack now functioned as a great tool because it kept me in balance and I used it as a brake several times. The weight of the wet sleeping bag provided more grip. When I slipped I would lean back and the pack would slow me down.

After one hour I found Warren's walking boots. Neatly stuck behind a few rocks and fittingly together as a couple. I fished them out of the water, tied the shoelaces together and placed them on a big boulder. The boulder was rising up out of a curve in the creek. If a rescue party was coming up they would not be able to overlook that strong symbol. I placed more cairns during the first few hours of my descent but gave up on that after a while because it kept disturbing my concentration and momentum. Often I had to manoeuvre very dangerously to place the piles of stones on the tops of landmarks and that lead to unnecessary tiredness and fear. Fear was the most energy-draining thing that happened to me on the journey.

Around 9.00am all hell broke loose above me. Once again the rainy season poured its afterbirth over me, and over Warren in his trap. 'Was this the revenge of Mother Nature for our risky operation?' I wondered. It rained so fiercely that I had to take off my glasses, which now made me visually handicapped. I sat in the tall grass way above the creek for a while. I put the hood of my raincoat over my head, cleaned my specs and looked into a curtain of water. Carefully I stored the glasses in my pack and continued my path.

There was no time to stop for a long break. Sometimes I would slip off a rock and fall in the creek. I carefully stuck to the sides. Sitting on the edge of a rock, up to my thighs in the water, I would cup my hands and drink from the water in front of me. Letting the liquid ease my tired body, then checking my wristwatch to see what time it was. I wore my plastic raincoat over a T-shirt and it made me sweat heaps so I had to drink all the time. But walking without it would have meant that I had no protection against the thorns and sharp plant growth in the jungle. I preferred the first option.

Whenever the creek was too dangerous I would go bush, but that always meant detouring around and through dense rainforest. And there was a risk that I would end up somewhere wrong. That happened a few times. I would bush-bash through the jungle only to find an even more dangerous situation further along. Once I walked into a nest of green tree ants. The bright green insects smelled of lemon and quickly found their way under my raincoat and T-shirt. They bit me all over my body, stopping only when I threw off my pack and jumped into a safe rock pool, my raincoat bulging, and frantically began to wash them off. The pain didn't last long and I didn't get sick.

The jungle

Short but tough climbing plants with razor-blade leaves, like a gigantic milled edge of a steak knife. Grasses, metres high, which I held onto if I slipped away while bush-bashing high above the banks of the creek, cutting the insides of my hands raw. I remember kicking the undergrowth, being angry at it, losing my balance and sliding down when my feet had lost all remaining grip.

Once I had a particularly scared moment when I fell straight into the water of the flooding creek. All I could think of as I slid down the rock into the white water was how not to break my ankles. I hurt my bum; and my pack, shorts and underpants got serious holes in them. But when I splashed into the water my feet found ground and I sat up to my groin in it. Tired and angry with myself for having lost my concentration and having opted for the easiest way down. Enough to kill myself! My heart was in my throat.

There were moments when I sat on a rock, checking my body and trying to ease the ever-pumping mental energy that went through me. Loudly talking to myself to stay calm; 'Quiet Geert, you have the time. Whether it's two, three or four o'clock before you arrive at the beach doesn't matter.' Every step I took I was confronted with Warren's purple socks which came out of the shafts of my rapidly deteriorating boots. There was a strong symbolism in that because not only did they serve a purpose but they kept me thinking of my trapped friend. I planned to ask him if I could keep them. Around my neck I wore a scarf from my girlfriend and deep inside my pack I carried Warren's address book, wrapped in plastic. He had asked me to contact his father at the address written in this book, and give to him the book if something happened to Warren.

Concentration was the key word for a safe descent. I hardly lost it and patiently I made my way down. Yesterday, Warren had found an old red T-shirt somewhere in the creek and had draped it across a big boulder. Obvious to see from either direction. When I approached it I felt very disappointed because I knew I still had to go a long way.

Sometimes I lost my sense of direction too. Had no idea if I had to go a long way or if I was getting closer to the beach. Sometimes I feared that I took a wrong side-creek but that was impossible.

There were plenty of young eucalypts, the same kind of tough trees that I had tried to get down the night before. But in the descent they proved good holds as I bush-bashed down, even if they did also house the green tree ants. I really started to hate all the water around me, and the branches that hit me in the face. In the Tassie wilderness I had laughed when some of the branches hit me. 'Part of the bushwalking experience,' I thought. But here it only added to the misery.

The branches and climbers delayed my trip considerably. I would trip over them often as the grass hid them. They loved to stick themselves in between the pack and my back, sometimes literally dragging me down to the ground if I was too optimistic and made ground too quickly. I was not allowed to go down fast! The piece of metal that had once been a proud Swiss army knife now served as a jungle cutter to cut the climbers in front of me. Lost my Therm-a-rest — bloody stupid of me! Warren and I had even talked about how I should put it inside my pack but I had strapped it to the side — only to lose it.

Another pitfall for the pig-headed bushwalker: imprudence is often punished in the wilderness. I must have walked past a great collection of native plants and wildlife but I never noticed it. All it seemed to have in common was that the plants were very sharp and threw water over me when I touched them. This was no bird watching trip!

The round, red rocks of granite made an impression also. During the ascent they had been grey and red but the water and rain had changed their colour to green–black, although 'Warren's rock' was grey and had white lichens on it. But the creek was littered with round, smoothed rocks, slippery beyond belief as they funnelled the water that came from the sky and the mountainsides. All sizes too. 'One for everyone,' I thought, very treacherously.

Sometimes I found myself in a situation where I felt decidedly unsafe. These were the most exhausting moments. I would sit down and look at the area in front of me, where a grey blanket of rain came down, blocking a good view. Carefully I'd check my position and look at the rocks or as an alternative an escape route up through the banks. There were two choices only. Dense rainforest versus rocks and water. What to do? Man, what a scene! I'd wipe my hand across my face and feel the one-week-old beard and would try to arrange my thoughts and possibilities.

On one occasion I let myself slide into the water up to my chest while holding on to some growth that hung down in the creek on the right-hand bank. Half a step at a time I shuffled through the mad water, covered by white foam, balancing on my toes while I checked for holes beneath me. The thought of spraining or damaging an ankle kept me very careful. I couldn't see the bottom and stepped on a few wobbly rocks, making the blood curdle in my veins. Wading chest deep in seemingly one long line of rock pools and waterfalls. Frightened to get stuck with my foot under some rock. Every time I seemed to panic about the situation the thought of the trapped Warren helped me to overcome it. 'No way, I'm not gonna make it,' I said to myself and would continue.

Always noise

In addition to the growth and the physical elements, the other thing I had to cope with was the noise! Unbearable at times. Nature had created the perfect acoustic arena for it on Hinchinbrook Island. I should avoid noise. Noise, of supermarkets, traffic, stereos, industry to name but a few doesn't go with me very well, often sparking tension. In our modern society we don't seem to be comfortable without it any more. A bad development.

After our ascent and the night spent with Warren sitting in the creek, my ears had grown accustomed to the noise. Often I had to go through tunnel like situations. The plants and trees above me looked for each other's company and it created a dark atmosphere. The noise was always there.

During the descent a complete symphonic orchestra accompanied me. I started to understand where composers get their inspiration! There would be a basic rhythm, which varied in tone with the circumstances of the terrain. Sometimes quiet and only in the background but often interrupted by angry soloists, wild trumpet play and the kettledrum. A hissing sound closely as I shuffled through the creek. Screaming when I walked through the bush. Never stopping and varying in its moods.

Sometimes I would be high above the creek, away from the worst of it, and would sit down. At the time I was not occupied with the noise because I had other more obvious things to overcome but the noise was always there and played a very important part in this tragedy. Of course it kept me awake and on edge as well. So the aftermath of the monsoon also had a very useful side to it. The noise prevented me from falling asleep. It kept me alert.

When it rained very hard in the bush it would have at least a little serenity and in a way it was very beautiful also. Monsoon rain tends to fall straight; and with the water hitting the canopy of the trees, the boulders and the surface of the creek, it would create a great 'blanket' of noise. A comfortable and massive 'hiss' came over the area when it hit the rocks, the water in the creek and plants. I had to take off my glasses and could no more sit and watch. So I was listening to it. No choices here. No button to turn to alter the pattern and level of cope-ability.

If I was lucky I would find a stretch of ground, perhaps a hundred metres or so, where the elements of nature had actually created some sort of pathway for me. I would come around one of the thousands of bends and there it was. Right there in front of my eyes the foliage would open up and there was a long horizontal slab of rock that I could walk on with no interference of bushes or stones. Indeed sometimes I could make useful ground. But there were moments when I was sure that the rocks would give grip, yet I slipped and only just managed to hold on to a branch. Mosses would grow over its pores and I would pick the mosses to walk over as it provided me with more grip. Of course it was also a matter of how my mind coped with it at that particular moment. Not always was I on edge and there would be a few moments when I was just not careful enough.

Noon

The rains stopped around noon and with it my tiredness came to the surface. The temperature quickly rose. Thin sun filtered through the clouds. So I sat down, ate a few muesli bars, rolled a cigarette (which I kept dry no matter what happened) and dragged all the nicotine and heat into my body until I almost burned my lips. It started to look like I would never be able to get down. A few times I'd fallen hard and I was bleeding all over my body. The water thinned the blood and it tasted sweet. Once again my legs started to shake but I managed to hold them still by putting my hands on the knees. Slowly, however, I started to succeed. At about 3.00pm I arrived at a place where there had been a bushfire. The undergrowth had been burned and I was finally able to make some ground quickly. There I discovered that we had lost our trail quite early the previous day as I found some markers on rocks and trees.

Nobody there

At 4.30pm I arrived at the lagoon. It had taken us eight and a half hours to get up, eleven for me to get down! The last hour of my walk, knowing that I was going to make it, had made me enormously tired and I could hardly walk by now. I strolled to the camp but found no one, to my disappointment. I would have liked to pass the torch on to another trekker who then could walk back to the starting point of the trek. But there was nobody, and due to the storm there were no fishing boats in the bay either.

Lethargically I decided that it didn't matter anyway. For the first time I doubted whether Warren was going to make it. I felt depressed. So I threw off my soaking wet pack and undressed myself. I walked to the ocean, where I washed my wounds with salt water, and examined my body; it looked pretty ugly. The bush-bashing especially had left its marks. My hands and fingers were completely cut open by the sharp plants that I had had to push aside or which I had held onto as I slipped down my slippery way. Carefully I put plasters and bandages around them. My eyelids were bleeding, knees and legs cut all over. I vomited in the sand. My glasses had received a few knocks as well. I took a little mirror out of my toilet bag and examined my face: one lens partially covered my eyebrows.

I hung my clothes, pack, sleeping bag and walking boots to dry on branches of scrub that edged the beach. The wind would take care of it. My shorts were ripped; underwear too; and my boots were also fit for the dump, with big holes in them and tears at the seams. Warren's purple socks also had holes in them.

With long dried palm leaves, driftwood and tree branches I started a big fire. Warren, always thinking up there, had given me his whistle and an empty aluminium bag from a wine cask. He had told me to make a fire, then blow the whistle and wave with the bag to attract fishing boats — if they were there, of course, which they weren't! Dressed in my sarong I walked out onto the beach of Little Ramsay Bay and sat down in the sand. I looked up at Mount Bowen. Its summit was obscured by white clouds.

Looking at the sky around me I noticed it was overcast but nowhere as thickly as near the mountain. That's where the clouds all gathered. I looked at the foothills in the foreground, sporadically bright green but mostly dark olive in colour. Where the hills ended the cliffs of Bowen rose up quite vertically. I expected Warren's position to be somewhere there but I wasn't certain about it. I'd been in such a thick jungle and was too occupied with getting down in one piece. There weren't any landmarks left in my mind. Up there it was green, noisy and wet.

There was no point in walking to the starting point of the trek today. Tourist boats would not come in any more so it was better for me to make camp and rest before hiking back there tomorrow morning. So I set up my tent, which took me half an hour instead of the normal five minutes, and prepared another pasta meal. In between these various tasks I moved about like a lethargic zombie. I was too tired and had to think too much about Warren to eat, and washed the food and cleaned the saucepan in the sea. I noted a big SOS in the logbook, which was also kept in the storage box. According to it, nobody had passed through the camp yesterday or today. I crawled inside the tent and tried to sleep on the sand, covered by my sarong. The fire was still going on the beach. I had thrown a big pile of wood on it.

DREAMS

The room is filled with a mass of seething, naked bodies, engaged in every sexual act imaginable. From amongst the throng a former lover appears and takes my hand, leading me out of the room. 'Hey! What's wrong with this room?' I protest as she leads me into another. Waiting for us on a huge bed is another woman, unfamiliar to me. I'm sat down on a chair beside the bed as Leena crawls slowly across to her playmate. Sitting back in my seat, I watch transfixed as they begin caressing and exploring each other's bodies. Just when I'm beginning to wonder whether I can remain a bystander any longer, Leena turns to me and smiles, beckoning me over with a single finger motion, as if to say, 'C'mon, what are you waiting for? Isn't this what you always wanted?'

I step forward to join them, heart pounding as I squeeze myself between. The three of us seem to mesh together, the heat from our bodies intense, almost burning. Our sweat mingling, we melt into one…Suddenly, we're alone, just Leena and I.

'Where…' I begin, only to be cut short with a finger to my lips.

'Shhhhhh. It's OK. That's not all you wanted, is it?' she asks provocatively.

Before I can answer, she begins to take me on a journey through all the sexual fantasies I've thought about but never had the guts to bring up — my own sexual repression I've always sought to deny. Suddenly, and very reluctantly, I'm snapped back to the present. Or am I?

Drifting in and out of sleep, the boundaries have become blurred until I can no longer distinguish between dreams and reality. This made my next dream all the more difficult to accept.

I'd become involved with a group of Chinese businessmen. These guys were incredible. They went about setting up business deals, trading in merchandise, shares, whatever. They used the power of illusion to scam people in any way they wished — from showing prospective buyers through a building that didn't exist, to luring corporate executives into schemes that couldn't possibly work. They used the power of positive thinking in such a way that, when they thought about something strongly enough, it became a reality not only for themselves but also for those they chose to wield their power over. No matter what the problem, these guys had an answer.

They taught me to use these skills also, within myself. I became involved in some amazing scams myself, but, more importantly, was left thinking — no, knowing — that I could really be out from under this rock at any time. The reality of being trapped drifted into the dream intermittently, not really seeming of great importance. All I had to do was think about it strongly enough, and I could be somewhere else. *Shit, I may not even be here anyway; it could just be a figment of my imagination.*

So realistic was this dream that when at first I still found myself to be trapped, I thought it was just a case of me not doing it properly, not being skilled enough in the art of the mind. So I'd try again and again, unwilling to accept the truth until, finally, the stark reality hit home. It was so real that I found myself utterly devastated when I finally accepted it had only been a dream.

You're dreaming mate. You're still here and you are not going anywhere. It didn't work. It was all bullshit!

I'm still here. How the hell can I still be here? How can it be true, I was so close?

I was almost out and now the escape route had been stolen from me. Tears came freely as I cried myself back to sleep, shattered and disillusioned, freezing cold.

RECESSION

The dreams had been so real, they had totally distorted my concept of time. When I woke to sunshine on Friday morning, I would have bet my balls it was Saturday. It must have been the different time settings in the dreams that did it. Whatever the reason, the thought of it actually being Saturday completely devastated me.

Noooooooooooo! Why is this happening? What have I done to deserve this?

The water! The water's dropped right away. Only a trickle flowed down the buttress upstream, no longer the foreboding sound it had been less than twelve hours before. The level in the creek around me had dropped so much, I wondered what I would do if it dropped any further. I'd have trouble filling my cup if it did. As it was, I now had to reach well out from my body to a pool deep enough to get a decent cupful. *What if it dries up completely? No, don't even think about it.*

After drinking my first cup of water for the day, I let my bladder relax and felt the hot urine flood over my thighs. It didn't even occur to me at first that I had to do it. I just did it, sitting there. It actually felt quite good, kind of liberating. To just sit there and let yourself go. Even better than pissing in a wetsuit. I could almost see the attraction for those who get their kicks out of so called 'water sports'. Almost.

The feeling in my legs hadn't really changed. I still felt like I could flex my left leg, even though I couldn't see it and had no idea of the extent of the damage done to it. As for the right, I wept loudly upon noticing the green spots on my very grey looking foot. The knee was still very swollen, with dry crusted blood around the gash just below the cap.

'*I'm going to lose that foot,*' I realised suddenly, chilled at the thought.

No, they'll be able to save it won't they? I can't lose it! Christ! What the hell's the other one like? Could it be as bad?

I pushed the repercussions from my mind, knowing somehow that I had far more important things to focus my energy on, like my immediate survival.

Helicopter!

The blue tarp comes out again and I have it ready for what seems like an eternity. Am I imagining things? It sounded closer this time, but still seems to be everywhere but here, near me.

Come on, I'm not over there for God's sake!

The hum fades into the distance and I let the tarp fall beside me. I can't believe the cruelty of the script writer in this drama — how he or she could be teasing me like this.

Am I hallucinating? Are they vultures sitting up in those trees? They're probably just dead branches but I don't recall seeing them yesterday. They're patiently waiting up there for me. Ready to move in as I become too weak to fight them off.

Having run out of paw-paw spears late yesterday, I bring out the bread and cheese. Taking a bite of the bread, a heavy German rye, I wince as it digs into my mouth, all dry and hard. It feels like sawdust in my mouth, sticking to the roof and the insides of my cheeks.

My saliva. I've got no saliva, that's what it is.

I fill my cup and, adding some water to the bread in my mouth, start chewing. It tastes awful, my face involuntarily screws up in revulsion. My guts churn, and it's not long before I'm overwhelmed by the familiar urge to eject the contents of my stomach. Leaning to my left as far as possible, trying not to get any on me as I spew, I feel like a pathetic old drunk. Some runs down my chin onto my jacket. I groan, then retch again. And then again, this time bringing up nothing but yellow bile. *God I feel sick. I don't like this. This is not a good sign.*

Becoming more lucid now, especially once I start vomiting, as it increases my dehydration. It's during one of these retching spells (I've spewed up nothing more than the little water I've drunk; food just won't stay down) that I notice the pool of blood spreading around my right foot. *What the hell is this? Why am I bleeding now? I can't start bleeding now, I would have started straight away, not now, after all this time!*

I feel the icy lump in the pit of my stomach as I realise how helpless I am to deal with this. I can't even reach my foot from here, can't even twist it to get some idea of where the blood's coming from. All I can do is look at it and hope like hell that it stops bleeding.

I'm still wondering about the cause of the bleeding, and my resultant fate, when a movement from under my foot catches my eye. *A yabby! A yabby is chewing into my foot!*

'Piss off!' As I yell out, it ducks away into the red cloud and I can't feel anything, don't know if it's still at my foot or what's happening.

'Mate, you're finished!'

Breaking a piece off one of the branches supporting my back, I position myself ready to strike with my new spear. Hours seem to pass before he makes his next appearance. I drive the spear forward.

'Take that, you bastard!'

He's too quick, darting back under my foot as my spear hits the water above him. Half an hour later, he's back again. Again, he's too quick for me. This is too bizarre. I feel like I'm in a movie again. This couldn't happen in real life!

Feeling drowsy again, I'm worried about what he's going to do when I'm asleep. If he's caused me to bleed this much already, what's going to happen when my feet get softer? And they are only going to get softer. Eventually, the flesh is going to be so waterlogged, it will just be falling off. Will that mean he'll be able to do enough damage to leave me bleeding to death if he gets in deep enough?

The thought sickens me. *No way!* Taking off my green cotton shirt, I wrap it around the end of my stick, reach down and try to wrap it around my foot. The first couple of times I couldn't get it tight enough, and it needs to be tight. It's not going to work if it just obscures his access from my view; before I can even contemplate sleep I've got to be fairly sure he can't get at my foot any more.

The cold is affecting me more now. My left hand has begun to become numb, my little finger curling involuntarily. I take this as a sure sign of my increasing hypothermia. *They've got to get here soon. I can't last another night like this.*

Shouldn't Geert have made it by now? Surely someone would have noticed me not being at the other end for my ferry pickup? How long will they wait before raising the alarm? They may wait until tomorrow before getting a ranger to walk through, depending on reports from other hikers as to our whereabouts.

I can't imagine any search beginning before noon tomorrow. I don't think I'll be around by then, not the way things are going now. I can't even hold water down any more, spewing it up and dry-retching for ages afterwards. It really is starting to look like this is it.

It's all over — no two ways about it.

ANTS

Just when it seemed that things couldn't possibly get any worse, I felt the sting at the top of my right thigh, almost in the groin. *Shit, what was that?* Reaching down quickly to rub the bite, I am faced with dozens of them — all over my legs and clothes.

Bloody ants! They're biting me. Piss off, I don't need this!

There were lots of them. As quickly as I could kill them they were replaced by others, just as angry. I carried on slapping at them whenever I was bitten, which was becoming more and more frequently, until the absolute horror of what was happening became apparent. Emerging from the far end of my rock was the trail of ants leading under the rock to me. Realising that they were actually forming a trail,

I followed them back to the remains of their nest which, until recently, had been behind a slab of rock on the gorge wall. Until I'd disturbed it, that is. Now they had to find a new spot to nest and they'd found one with a ready food supply. *Me! They're moving their nest over to me! No! This can't be happening.*

This wasn't just any movie I'd ended up in. It was one of those weird, art-house movies, like something David Lynch would come up with. Horrific visions of dead animals covered with ants filled my mind, visions anyone who has spent any time watching them would be familiar with. The ants attacking a much larger animal, using sheer strength of numbers, invading the body openings first. The prey writhes in pain, unable to run away any more, the ants just niggling away in great numbers, eating their way into the ears and eyes of their victims before carving out their insides, leaving at first just the skin frame, then eventually only the clean, white bones.

Repellent! I've got some repellent in my first aid kit, left over in a tube I picked up in Kenya. Should be toxic enough for them.

I'd avoided using the repellent until now, being highly suspicious of its active ingredients. Unscrewing the cap quickly, I began rubbing it into the tops of my thighs, as far down as I could get. Then across into my groin, as far as I could reach. *You're not getting in there you little bastards!*

Next, I rubbed it all through my hair, then around my ears. Finally, I rubbed it as close as I safely could around my eyes.

I felt so cold and tired but knew I couldn't afford to go to sleep. With the yabby, the ants and the danger of hypothermia present, I had to try to stay awake. The repellent didn't really stop them from biting into my legs, but it did seem to keep them off my face. But it was no use: I just could not keep my eyes open. Unable to resist any longer, I succumbed, and began to drift in and out of sleep. Into dreams so real, they melded with reality.

I am floating, looking down at Geert talking to someone. He's in the ranger's office, relaying what's happened, that we need help urgently. I can see the ranger nodding his head, but he doesn't really believe Geert's story. 'We'll sort it out mate,' he reassures Geert, then arranges a helicopter for the search. He flies the mission alone, making a half-hearted attempt at a search. He doesn't really believe I'm out here, thinks the story is just some lack of communication between some tourist who can't speak English. He doesn't fly anywhere near me and returns back to his office to get on with the more important task of paperwork.

Have I just been dreaming? Could that be true? Could I really have just seen that?

It was so real, I knew I had to do something, to let him know it was true, that there *is* somebody out here. I consciously tried to travel out of my body, to get to him. I saw myself floating above the treetops, across ridges and valleys, then into his office. I didn't want to freak him out with my presence, putting myself into his head as if speaking directly with his conscience.

'Mate, there's somebody out there. You've got to go and have another look. The guy wasn't bullshitting you — there really is somebody out there. Just below the summit of Mount Bowen, in Warrawilla Creek. Please go and have another look.'

With that, I returned, satisfied that I'd tried. *You gave it your best shot, mate.*

I opened my eyes with the bizarre feeling of not knowing whether I'd been dreaming or not. It was all so real. Maybe I was still dreaming.

The day was drawing to a close. There was nothing else I could do but sit and wait for darkness to arrive. I began to feel cold again, my left hand totally clawed now, with my right numb as well. I tried speaking, to see whether my speech had become slurred (the next stage of hypothermia) but it sounded OK.

This didn't give me any reassurance, though. I'd all but given up. I was really only waiting to die. The vultures were still waiting in the gum downstream.

So this is what it's like to die slowly, all alone, out in the bush. It doesn't feel as glamorous as I thought it would. Maybe because it's taken so long.

My mind drifted back to another time and place, when I'd met someone who could have related to how I felt now. Someone staring death in the face.

ROGER

In the north-west corner of Tasmania is an area known as the Tarkine. It is a wild land, shaped to a degree by the wild weather it is subjected to. The coast is hammered by wind pushed across the Southern Ocean by the roaring forties combined with huge ocean swells. Behind huge coastal sand dunes, button grass plains flow inland, fifteen kilometres to the foothills of the Norfolk range. Meandering rivulets carry the average three metres of annual rainfall through temperate rainforest, then tea-tree scrub before depositing the now tannin-stained water into the ocean.

I first heard of the Tarkine while staying with friends in the north-eastern corner of Tasmania, friends I'd met in Germany four years earlier and had contacted again on my arrival in February 1995. Christine and Ebehard Haas live in a small town called Weldborough, about two hours' drive east of Launceston. In the peace and tranquillity of the Blue Tiers and the Weld Valley, they had raised four children. Seppi, Carl, Eleanor and Lara learned from an early age to respect their environment, encouraged to entertain themselves in the natural surroundings.

Ian Matthews, a good friend of Christine and Ebi, worked for the Wilderness Society. Ian told me one night of the tragedy that was occurring in the north-west; of how the Tasmanian government, against the advice of the federal environment minister, had begun construction of a road through the heart of the Tarkine wilderness. Cutting through part of the largest tract of temperate rainforest in the Southern Hemisphere, the road would cross one of Tasmania's wildest rivers, the Donaldson. I'd been amazed, in my short time spent in the state, at the extent of logging operations. And I'm not talking about timber harvested from pine plantations; huge trucks careered around the state carting logs of native timber, some of them from trees so huge that only two or three would fit on a truck.

I couldn't believe my eyes driving towards Cradle Mountain, Tasmania's premier tourist destination, that a huge area of forest had been clear-felled right beside the road! What kind of a message is that to be giving to people who come from all over the world to revel in what their own countries lost long ago? Nature. Wild nature. We've got it, and look what we're doing to it.

Ian's insistence that this was the biggest environmental concern since the Franklin River campaign had me more than intrigued. I'd become concerned about what we were doing to our wilderness areas, how they were being developed and tamed — effectively, disappearing. I decided that I had to go and have a look for myself and see what exactly was happening in this 'Tarkine'.

From the moment I arrived, I was captivated. I had never been in rainforest like it. Dark, primeval forest, standing now, as it had for thousands of years. Often, as I sat quietly in places that I'm sure had never seen another human being, a sense of timelessness filled me. Unable to walk away from the destruction I witnessed, I joined the protesters. Over the ensuing months, we developed into a tight-knit group, labelled by the media as 'The Tarkine Tigers'. We had established ourselves in the forest, determined to carry out our role of custodians, to keep the area wild and free for ourselves and future generations.

As winter approached, we realised the need to maintain a constant vigil in the Donaldson River valley. We had been assured that construction would be put on hold until spring. But a few months earlier, given similar assurances, we had left the valley, only to find that contractors had made a full scale push in our absence. In an effort to gain as much ground as possible, they made a beeline across the button grass plains, trashing each band of forest encountered. Up until then, they had been slowly moving forward, building the road as they went. Now, they were determined to cut right through to the very heart of the Tarkine: the Donaldson River and its surrounding rainforest. We were determined to stop them, and weren't taking any chances. We would maintain a presence in the forest over winter, basing a crew in the bush on a weekly roster.

My shift had come around again. Leaving Weldborough early one frosty morning, I again drove across the state, for the umpteenth time, to the small mid-western town of Nabageena. Paul Clarke and Michelle Foale lived in a house Paul had built on a small piece of land. Surrounded by plantation forest and farmland, he had maintained an oasis of natural bushland. Paul had offered to drive me in to our drop-off point on the Tarkine's fringe. He was to pick up a group of young guys, in on their first visit, so we could kill two birds with one stone. First, though, we had to detour to the west's largest town, Smithton (or 'mifton, as it was affectionately known amongst us). We had to pick up a guy named Jarrah who would be coming into the forest for the first time. I always enjoyed taking people on their first visit to the Tarkine. Seeing the wonder in their eyes, knowing they were experiencing something magical.

Finding Jarrah wasn't a problem. When you've got dreadlocks like his, Smithton is not an easy place to hide in! With the three of us squashed into the front of Paul's ute, we filled Jarrah in on what had been happening so far. He had been quite actively involved with the North East Forest Action Group, (NEFA) in New South Wales. He'd seen plenty of forest action before, and had heard on the grapevine what was happening in the Tarkine. He'd come down to see it first hand, then work out what he could do to help.

An hour and a half later, where the forestry road became no more than a dirt path, we reached the beginning of our secret access track. It allowed us to get large numbers of people into the area without detection. Waiting for us there, cold and wet, were the four guys to be picked up. They were still running on a high from their experience, being in such a wild place. Eyes wide, they assured us we wouldn't believe how hard it was walking in there. I looked at Paul, smiling as I replied, 'I reckon I might have a bit of an idea.'

'How come there's only four of you? Isn't there supposed to be five?' asked Paul, looking concerned.

One member of the previous party, a guy called Roger, had decided to stay in the bush for another week. He would have been on his own for a few days before the next group — these guys — arrived, leaving with them the following week. Maybe he'd wanted to stay for another shift…

'We heard there was going to be someone there already, but we never saw them. We found a sleeping bag and some other stuff at the camp, but there was no sign of anybody,' one of them recalled.

'Shit! Did you look for him at all?' asked Paul.

'Yeah, we walked around calling out for ages but eventually figured that he must have left,' someone else replied.

'Why would he leave behind all his gear like that?' I questioned, knowing the obvious answer, but trying to understand *their* reasoning.

The statement of what I knew came from Paul: 'If he'd gotten himself lost or injured,' he said gravely.

We all stood in silence as the magnitude of the situation began to sink in.

'We need to get in there straight away,' I said to Paul, looking to Jarrah for his approval. This wasn't going to be the walk in the park that we'd planned. We were going to have to get in and out as fast as possible.

'I'll meet you back here at the same time tomorrow night,' Paul added. 'If you're not here, I'm going to have to call the police to organise a search party.'

'Try ringing around in Hobart first,' I replied. 'He may have walked out and be sitting in a café in Hobart right now.'

'OK. You blokes'd better get moving. It's late. I'll be on the phone as soon as I get home and see what I can find out,' he replied, tying the tarp down to head off.

Jarrah and I adjusted our packs and climbed the log that hid the beginning of our track.

'Good luck!' Paul called out behind us, and we were on our way.

The track we used had been cut a few months earlier and was difficult to follow in places. Our progress slow despite the steady pace we kept, we were still in the forest as the sun began to set and walked out onto the button grass plain in near darkness. Having erected the tent almost half a metre off the ground on a cushion of button grass, we had a quick meal of pasta, climbed into the tent and settled into our sleeping bags, tired after our strenuous walk.

As the first rays of light crept across the plain, we wolfed down breakfast, Jarrah's eyes open wide at his first glimpse of the Tarkine. The button grass plains spread out below, cut by fingers of forested valleys running down from the slopes of the Norfolk range in the distance. Standing out markedly was the ugly white scar of the road under construction, cutting across the plains, breaking the pristine landscape.

After packing up camp, we set off again, soon dropping into the first of many gullies that made travelling difficult. Filled with waist high heath and cutting grass, these gullies slowed our progress considerably, but we pushed on. On reaching the road, we found little relief as we struggled along what had turned into a continuous quagmire. 'How in the hell are they going to maintain this?' I asked myself, standing knee deep in mud.

Hours later we reached the opening cut into the tall forest leading down into the Donaldson valley. Just inside, we left the road and made our way through the huge gums to our bark hut camp. Forrest and Ben had built the hut a month earlier and it was a work of art. Jarrah was still admiring their handiwork, and the extent of our establishment, when I noticed, above the wind whistling through the trees, the sound of a helicopter approaching.

'C'mon mate,' I said to Jarrah, as I began heading back to road, beckoning him to follow. 'I don't want them to know about this place unless they really need to.'

Four figures appeared at the rise, walking down towards us. I immediately recognised one as Paul, and my stomach dropped as the implications became obvious. The three others all looked like cops. Sure enough, as they reached us, Paul, looking even more serious than he had the night before, said to me, 'He's not in Hobart, Wazza. Nobody's seen him, mate.'

'Shit!' was all I managed to say before one of the cops stepped forward and, without even introducing himself, said, 'OK, you guys are going to help us search for this guy. You shouldn't be in here anyway, but since you are, you're going to show us every one of your little hiding places. Every camp. Everything! If I find out that you've held out on us, there'll be all hell to pay!'

'Mmmm. You've made that fairly clear,' I thought to myself.

'Now, where are we going to start?' he barked.

'The others say they found his sleeping bag at the camp down closer to the river,' I replied.

'Let's go then,' the chief ordered, and we all started towards the Donaldson.

As we walked, calling out the whole time, the officer in charge kept reminding us of how much trouble we'd be in if we didn't cooperate fully.

Leading them straight to the Donaldson River campsite, I reflected on the measures we'd taken to keep its location secret. Covering our tracks whenever we came or went had paid off when the police had tried to find our camp. Sending two officers on foot through the original survey track, looking for footprints, they had found nothing. Now we had to lead them directly to it.

Seeing Roger's bedding laid out under the tarp, his pack alongside, drove home the reality of what was happening here. Butterflies invaded my stomach as I thought of all the possibilities. He could have slipped and injured himself in some way. He could easily have become lost.

We split up and began searching around the vicinity of the camp. I'd begun looking for a body. Anyone out in this sort of weather without warm clothes or a sleeping bag wouldn't have lasted long, I'd decided. Peering under logs, brushing aside clumps of bracken, I expected a corpse to stare back at me at any moment. We were running out of light now.

One of the rescue guys used our tree ladder to gain some height so he could radio their chopper. Ironically, we had built it to spot helicopters. These were being used to drop contractors with chainsaws directly into the forest, so we had to know where. As soon as we knew one was landing, we would race to the area and make our presence known. They were under orders to stop work if any protesters were in the area, for safety reasons.

'I know of one more place to look,' I suggested. 'Down at the river they've been dropping some pretty big trees. It's dangerous in there, the trees haven't settled yet, anything could happen.'

'OK, you've got 15 minutes,' the chief said to Jarrah and me. 'Take this with you.' And he handed Jarrah a hand-held two-way radio. He briefly explained how to use it, then, as we turned to leave, added, 'If you guys disappear on me, there'll be hell to pay!' Paul stayed with the police to help them search the original survey track, which we still used in preference to the road.

Scouring the hillside above the swathe of fallen trees, we called out constantly, though I was still sure it was a body we were looking for. The helicopter had been circling overhead. As we approached the clearing, it sounded like it was landing. We were moving as quickly as possible, but progress was still agonisingly slow through the dense under-storey. We looked at each other in surprise as the drone of the helicopter's engine turned into a high pitched whine and it lifted off! Minutes later, we reached the clearing. Nobody else was in sight.

'What do you think they're doing?' I asked Jarrah.

'I don't know, mate,' he replied. 'Maybe they've gone back up onto the button grass.'

After waiting five minutes, we began making our way up to meet them, Jarrah calling down into the gully below for any sign of Roger. 'Cooooooooooeeeee!' then stopping, listening for a reply. I really thought he was wasting his time. *He's dead. There's no way he'd still be alive if he's been lost all this time.*

Suddenly, Jarrah stopped in front of me. 'Did you hear that?', he whispered, frowning.

'Did I hear what?'

'Listen,' he said, then called again. 'Cooooooooooeeee!'

I strained my ears, trying to hear anything above the wind hissing through the trees. Nothing.

'Did you hear that?' he asked excitedly, looking into my eyes for confirmation.

'No. I didn't hear anything, except for the wind,' I replied, sure he was imagining things.

'I'm sure I heard something. Listen again,' he pleaded, then he called even louder this time: 'Cooooooooooeeee!'

Standing with my head cocked to one side, left ear facing down into the gully, my heart skipped a beat as I heard the faint reply.

'Did you hear that?' Jarrah grabbed my arm.

'I did, mate. I heard something.' My heart was racing. We both called out this time and, sure enough, heard the faint reply again.

'He's alive!' I announced out loud, betraying my disbelief.

We then took a bearing of the direction his voice came from: fifty-eight degrees from where we stood. At that moment, Paul appeared, cresting a small rise in the track.

'We've found him!' Jarrah and I both yelled out at once, much to Paul's astonishment.

'Where are the coppers?' I asked Paul. He explained that they'd flown back to Savage River, unable to wait for us any longer.

'That's the shortest 15 minutes I've ever seen!' I replied in amazement.

'The radio,' Jarrah exclaimed, holding it up. 'We can get them on this!'

Being on a hillside in mountainous terrain, the radio replied with nothing but static.

'I've got to get to higher ground,' he announced. 'Then I should be able to get a signal.'

'We've got to get down there,' said Paul, looking to me and receiving agreement. 'We need to get him some food and warm clothing.'

'In the dark?' Jarrah queried, sounding concerned, the sun now below the horizon.

'I'm not going to be able to just lie down and sleep now that I know he's down there,' I snapped.

'I know that, but you haven't stopped all day. At least have something to eat before you go,' he reasoned. Jarrah had a point. I was running on adrenaline only, and that doesn't last forever.

Looking down into the gully one last time, I tried to imagine what must be going through this guy's mind. How he must have felt as he realised we'd heard him; and now, when we were leaving again. Would he realise that we would be coming straight back? Would he resign himself to another night alone, comforted, albeit slightly, that he'd been found, that he would be saved?

Jarrah ran ahead, hoping to get a message to the chopper before it was too far away. Paul and I went back to the bark hut and began putting together the equipment we'd need. Paul cooked some pasta and soup to take with us in a Thermos and I ran out to the road and up the hill to the button grass looking for Jarrah. I found him at the top of the next rise, in a scene I'll never forget.

In an effort to gain more height, he'd dragged a discarded 44-gallon drum into the centre of the road and stood it on end. Balancing precariously on top of it, he announced loudly and slowly into the radio held against his ear, 'Hobart! Hobart! This is bark hut rescue, do you read me? Over.'

Amongst the static, a barely discernible voice could be made out, but Jarrah was unsure whether they had received his message.

'It's no use, mate. They're not going to be able to do anything anyway, not until morning,' I reminded him. 'Paul and I are going down there.'

'OK,' he replied. 'Good luck.'

As I raced back into the forest I could still hear 'Hobart! Hobart!'

Standing on the thin survey track looking down into the darkness below, I felt like I was about to embark on a night dive. We were on the side of a ridge that dropped down at about 45 to 60 degrees through

Photo: Warren Macdonald

Using a self-timer, I took this shot in the prehistoric atmosphere of the Ruwenzori Mountains, the so-called 'Mountains of the Moon' bordering Uganda and Zaire.

Top: The stunning beauty of the Tarkine wilderness.

Bottom: Just a few of the courageous Tarkine forest defenders. From left: Claire, Michael (back), Georgie, Pippin, Be, Alanna, Russell (back), Forrest and Polly. Taken at the Donaldson River base camp in March 1995.

Above: This is public transport, Zairean-style. I travelled on top of this truck for three days between Bukavu and Kamituga, Zaire in September and October 1992.

Left: The main road from Bukavu to Kindu, Zaire. President Mobutu was one of the world's richest men, yet he spent nothing on services outside his own province.

Photo: C & D Frith

The majestic summit of Mount Bowen, Hinchinbrook's tallest peak.

Top: Geert took this photo after our tortellini dinner on the night of April 9th, about twenty minutes before I took my last step.

Bottom: The scene greeting paramedic Chip Jaffurs as he reaches me in fading light. Hinchinbrook Island, April 11th 1997.

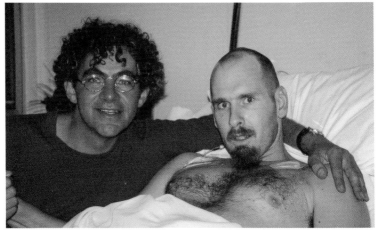

Photo: Graeme Macdonald

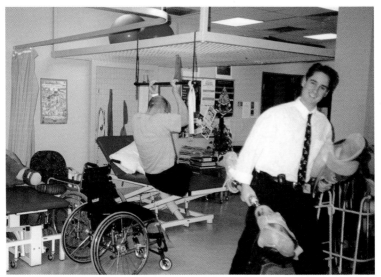

Photo: Helen Connor

Top: With Geert van Keulen in Cairns Base Hospital, early May 1997. Note the morphine-induced 'Charles Manson' look.

Bottom: Working out on a custom built chin up bar at the amputee gym, Royal Talbot Rehabilitation Centre, while prosthetist Tim Jarrott escorts my legs to the parallel bars for more walking training.

Photo: Graeme Macdonald

Photo: Daphne Smith

Walking for the first time outside hospital in the backyard at Mum and Dad's in December 1997.

Celebrating after the Lorne 'Pier to Pub' open water swim, January 10th 1998.

Photo: Graeme Macdonald

Sanding back a bench seat for painting at Mum and Dad's. Simple jobs like this helped me realise that I had lost a hell of a lot, but not everything.

Photo: Cate Weate

Photo: Cate Weate

Sunset on the summit of Cradle Mountain, January 31st 1998. From left: Eddie Storace, Ian Matthews and myself.

Negotiating the boulder-strewn slopes of Cradle Mountain with Michael Croll.

Photo: Jeremy Smith

Gaining altitude the hard way. Cradle Mountain.

dense rainforest. The torch beam, which we used to look for an opening, failed to penetrate more than a few metres into the tangle.

I pulled down hard on my shoulder straps, drawing the pack tightly in to my back, and looked across at Paul. He nodded his readiness.

Setting the compass bearing at 58 degrees, I stepped forward. 'OK, this is it. Let's do it.'

We literally dropped off the side into the dark before being stopped almost immediately by the first barrier of scrub, known as 'horizontal'. Horizontal, as the name implies, grows horizontally. And vertically. And every angle in between! It creates an almost impenetrable web, tangled amongst itself in the forest under-storey. Climbing through it carefully, we made our way forward. With the strap firmly around my wrist, the torch swung free whenever I had to use both hands, beam dancing wildly across the ferns and moss beneath my feet. I'd become accustomed to moving through this type of terrain over the last few months. At first, I'd been completely freaked out by it. Now, we were on a mission.

Stopping to check the compass and pick out our next landmark, I called out 'Coooooooooeeeee!'

The response was immediate, clearer now that the wind had died down. Urged on by this, we moved quickly forward, sometimes falling as rotting logs gave way. In sections the forest opened up, allowing us to move faster. Roger's response became louder and louder as we moved closer. Calling continuously, we were talking to him now, telling him it was OK, that we had him.

We would have been less than a kilometre from the track when we finally reached him. Calling out again, his response came from right in front of me. But it wasn't till I leant down that I saw him. Staring back at me with wild eyes, he reminded me of a scared, wounded animal.

'Mate. Am I glad to see you!' I sighed as I worked my pack off. Reaching under the log, I took his arm. It was soaking wet, and cold. Since hearing the helicopter this afternoon, he had been standing in the river (which was just below us now), trying to attract attention.

No sooner had we'd introduced ourselves than he staggered me by asking, 'Have you guys got any tobacco? I could do with a smoke.'

'No, we haven't, mate. But I've got some hot soup here if you'd like some.'

As he sipped the hot soup, we asked him what had happened, how he had ended up down here. He had left one of our campsites (we had several), to get some coffee from another. As it was imperative that we stay hidden in the forest, we were all very careful to avoid leaving any tracks that could alert the police to our whereabouts. Roger had simply become disoriented between the two camps, and soon found himself lost. For days he had wandered, attempting to find his way back, but to no avail. With only a handful of oats in one pocket, he'd been too scared to eat until he really needed to. Eventually finding the log, he'd been sheltering under it for a couple of days before hearing the helicopter. It was now a full eight days since he'd set out to get the coffee, and he still had the oats in his pocket!

At first, I was amazed at how casual Roger was about the whole situation, and left Paul to tend to him while I started looking for a place to pitch the tent. I realised later that he must have had to raise himself incredibly to deal with his seemingly hopeless situation. He had convinced himself that he was OK, rather than face the soul-destroying reality of dying cold and alone under a sodden log.

Using a tomahawk, I cleared a space within the web of horizontal through the under-storey. Barely big enough for the tent, it was at least on the most even ground available. I somehow squeezed it into the small space, by which time Paul had set Roger up with a cup of hot soup. His feet looked terrible, swollen and cut from walking in bare feet. He hadn't worn any shoes, preferring to go barefoot as he always did. But now that choice had turned against him. The Tasmanian bush is a lot more extreme, and the constant damp in the rainforest would have softened his feet more than usual. He had wrapped them in what looked like the sleeves of his shirt, but they had been cut so badly that the blood had seeped through.

He agreed to come out from under the log, reluctantly; it must have given him some kind of comfort and he was apprehensive about giving it up. We both half-carried him over to the tent, Paul crawling inside with him to arrange his sleeping bag. I spread my sleeping bag out in the gap under Roger's log, then crawled into it for what was, up to that point, one of the worst night's sleep of my life. I couldn't believe this guy had lasted so long under there. I was soaking wet within half an hour. Luckily I had a Dacron sleeping bag, or I would have frozen! I tossed and turned all night, feeling completely claustrophobic with the dank underside of the log only centimetres from my face. I felt humbled by the experience, almost like I *had* to sleep under there. *He's been under here for that long with only the clothes on his back. Surely I can handle one night.*

Inside the tent, Paul spent all night huddled up to Roger, hugging him to keep him warm. Paul had feared that he might lose him when he slipped into a fever as he warmed up, his body shivering uncontrollably.

I woke from my semi-sleep at first light to the sound of a chopper. Racing down to the river, I stepped out onto the slippery rocks and waved my arms to flag it down. They spotted me immediately and, after circling a few more times, proceeded to winch the first of three crew down onto a tongue of rock. It made an incredible sight, the giant steel hummingbird hovering perfectly still between the trees on either side of the river. As soon as the bloke on the line touched down, he unclipped, signalled to the 'bird' above, and made his way over the treacherous rocks to where I stood on the bank. He introduced himself as a paramedic, and enquired after Roger's whereabouts and condition.

'Follow me, he's just up here.' And I led him back up the steep bank.

As he tended to Roger, the officer in charge appeared, and he wasn't happy.

'What happened to you guys yesterday? Didn't I tell you not to disappear?' he barked.

Angry at his accusation, I replied, 'You didn't wait for us. That's the shortest 15 minutes I've ever seen.'

'And what did you think you were doing coming down here in the dark like that? Look at the danger you've put yourselves in! We could have ended up searching for you as well this morning!' he ranted.

'We've been in here for months, mate! Do you think we would have come down here if we didn't think we could do it? Look at the gear we've brought down with us.' If he was furious with us, I was furious too — with his attitude.

When he'd stepped away shortly after, the paramedic turned to me and said, 'Don't take too much notice of him, mate. You guys did the right thing and you did it well. Don't worry about what he says, he's just pissed off at the whole episode. As far as I'm concerned, you guys have done the rescue, we're just taking him out now.'

Paul and I stood back, feeling much better at the recognition of our efforts, as the paramedic went about stabilising Roger, getting him ready for the stretcher. He was in a lot worse condition than had first been apparent, suffering badly from exposure and hypothermia. I don't think he would have lasted much longer where he was. After he'd been strapped into the fibreglass stretcher, we all helped carry him down the steep bank to the river, across the slippery rocks beneath the helicopter hovering overhead.

As Roger was lifted up into the waiting bird, then whisked away, I began retracing my steps up the steep slope, through the bracken and dogwood to our makeshift camp. Quickly packing up the tent, I stuffed everything into my pack, ready for a quick escape. Our work had finished here.

'I'll see you guys later on. You don't need me any more,' I announced. I knew Paul would have to go back in the chopper, not having his pack, but I wanted to get back to the camp.

'Where do you think you're going?' the angry one barked.

'I've got to go back and pick up some gear, do a few things,' I replied.

'Not that way you're not,' he snaps.

'Why not?' I ask, truly angry now, 'How do you think I got here?'

'I don't care, mate. I can't let you go back that way. What if something happens to you? How good is that going to look for us?' he tells me, obviously enjoying himself.

'Hey, I came down there in the dark, mate. I reckon I might be able to get back in broad daylight!' I replied sarcastically.

'Forget it! You're coming with us!'

Jesus! It wasn't as if we were under arrest or anything. And we had found Roger after they'd shot through!

The others were beginning to make a move down towards the riverbank now, and I saw this as my chance to do the bolt. But Hitler stood waiting for me. 'C'mon mate, we're leaving.'

'Yeah, I'll be down there in a sec, mate. I'm just going to have a piss,' I replied moving over to an appropriate spot.

This was my chance. I had my pack on. *As soon as I've had this piss,*
I'm out of here.

I turned to find him standing right beside me, waiting.

'You right there, mate?' I enquired.

'Finish your piss and let's go.'

I still wanted to make a run for it, just take off into the bush. But my
pack was heavy with all the extra gear we'd brought along for Roger.

He may be a slow fat bastard, but I'm not going to be able to move through
this horizontal too quickly with a heavy pack on.

'Yeah, all right,' I replied, agitated that he had me. He followed me
down to the riverbank all the way, and I began to regret having not run
for it immediately.

The chopper eventually returned from depositing Roger and each
of us was winched up into it.

The forest looked incredible from up in the air, seeming to go on
forever. I was mesmerised by the colours. I'd never seen so many varia-
tions of green, individual trees standing out distinctly in the crowd.

Then, on the horizon, *Jesus Christ!* A huge piece of forest had been
ripped up like a piece of turf. Before us yawned the gaping hole of the
Savage River mine. As we got closer I peered down into the toxic
green tailings dams below, the ones that occasionally run straight into
the Savage River. Huge machines tore away at the earth as I watched,
and the enormity of our struggle loomed gloomily.

We truly are living in a world gone mad. Why have we got no respect for the
earth? Why have we got no connection?

When did we lose it? This question filled my head as we descended
towards a large service station car park in the township of Savage
River.

Paul and I received the full-on interrogation at the local police station before being driven in to Burnie for more of the same. As I
stepped out of the police Landcruiser in the heart of Burnie, the officer
looked me up and down, smiling, 'So, do you always come into town in
your underwear?'

I hadn't progressed to polypropylene at that stage, making do with a
pair of long-johns I'd picked up for a few dollars.

'Yeah, no worries mate. I'm not really supposed to be in town,
remember!' I replied, sick of this whole situation. We hadn't done

anything wrong, and we were being treated like criminals. I felt a deep sadness that this is what we had come to, our so called 'civilised' society. The very fact that we had to be out there at all appalled me. As I explained to a hostile woman in a Burnie pub one afternoon, I had better things to do with my life. I'd rather be getting on with living than go through confrontation after confrontation, my spirit being beaten into the ground. But I, like all the others, simply couldn't stand by after seeing what was happening in there. We had been deeply moved by nature, and treated like criminals for heeding its call.

Thinking about this whole episode later, I began to realise what I'd gained from the experience. It had reinforced in me my competence in the wild. Jumping off that track with Paul was like crossing into another realm, and he felt it too. We had gone to the outer limits of our comfort zones in order to bring back again someone who was even further out. And to see first hand the resilience of the human spirit, the way Roger had raised himself mentally to survive. He had to believe he was OK, otherwise he would have just slipped into the void, slowly going mad, or becoming hysterical at the enormity of his situation. Talking himself up was the only way he could have held himself together. I had experienced a fraction of his ordeal in sleeping under his log.

They were important lessons to learn, more important than I could have ever possibly imagined. Lying under 'my' rock years later, it would be these experiences that I would draw upon. Knowing I was strong enough. That I'd been tested before. Knowing I had to hold it together to keep myself from slipping into that same black void that Roger had been staring into when we found him under that log.

FOUND
Helicopter.

Am I still dreaming? Am I still alive? Can I hear a helicopter?

It sounds like it's getting louder.

Yes!

Instantly awake again now, I feel my heart begin to pound. I grab the poly tarp and quickly unfold it, my eyes frantically scanning the sky for a sign. The noise is getting louder.

Please God, let it be looking for me.

Suddenly, out of the blue sky, looking like a dragonfly in the distance, a helicopter.

Yes, they're looking for me! Yes!

My heart must have been pounding at 130 beats per minute.

Over here! I'm over here!

Holding the tarp up high, waving it steadily back and forth so as to keep it at its maximum size, I pray for them to come closer. For, even though I can see them, I know from past experience with helicopters that they would find it difficult seeing me down in this gully. They are going to need to be directly over me, and they are far from that at the moment, apparently following another gully to the south-east of me. Finally, they're heading this way, until eventually they pass almost directly over me at a height of about fifty metres.

'Here! I'm down here!' But they keep going, checking another gully to the north-east, over towards 'the thumb'.

Then they're off, heading towards the coast. Filled with elation and despair, I still don't know whether they've seen me or not.

They should have circled me, shouldn't they?

I struggle with the concept of them not seeing me before realising: *They're looking for me. Of that I'm certain!*

The next five or ten minutes are the longest of my life, before the giant insect appears again, this time heading straight towards me. It stops directly above, swirling tree litter and debris all around me before tilting forwards and swooping into a wide circle. I can see someone at the window inside.

Are they giving me the thumbs up? They circle again before turning to leave.

Where the bloody hell are they going?

It doesn't matter, they've seen me. I slump back on my Therm-a-rest as if a huge weight has been lifted from my shoulders, the chopper heading back towards the coast. No matter what happens now, I'm no longer alone.

THE RESCUE

The sight of the returning helicopter was one that will stick me forever... flying directly towards me this time, circling once before taking up a position a hundred metres downstream; hovering perfectly, like a giant dragonfly over one of the few clear sections on the river. The wind generated was incredible. I could only sneak quick glances as leaves, dust and water were blown up the gully, the wind roaring along with the beating and chopping of the rotor blades. I was fully aware of just how dangerous this was and closed my mind to thoughts of anything else going wrong.

Catching glimpses of another human being lowered into the middle of the creek bed, I felt so grateful for technology. He looked so professional, walking carefully towards me, checking me out as would a hunter approaching a wild animal — assessing the situation, noting my signs.

'My name is Chip Jaffurs. I'm a doctor,' he shouts, his American accent unmistakable above the roar of the rotors. 'How are you doing?'

'I'm all right mate. Fuck, am I glad to see you.'

Chip crouches down beside me, setting his plastic case on some rocks alongside. Later I learn that he is an emergency medicine specialist, having worked in the field for over ten years. Opening his case as we speak, he begins with the first of many questions.

'Are you in pain?'

'No,' I reply. 'Not any more.'

'How long have you been here?'

'Since Wednesday.'

'When did you last eat?'

'Yesterday, I think. I've been throwing up all day.'

'When did you last drink?'

'This morning?' I answer with a question to myself.

'Are you allergic to any drugs?'

'No, none that I know of.'

Finding my blood pressure down at 60 systolic, which is extremely low — a product of dehydration and shock, he begins putting together an intravenous line with a needle the size of a knitting needle. It stings sharply as it pushes, rather than slides, in. Through the line he firstly introduces morphine, followed by antinausea medication to try to control my vomiting. He then washes the ants off my legs with cups of water. I've long forgotten about them, but apparently they've been having quite a picnic. A wave of warmth and well-being sweeps over me as the morphine takes hold.

The chopper has been hovering just downstream, winching crewman Dany Portefaix and airport fire officer Bill Johnstone down into the creek. They have with them hydraulic lifting equipment, a crowbar and a couple of stepped wooden blocks. With all the gear off-loaded, the helicopter leaves the scene, returning to the beach to conserve fuel. Helicopters are notorious for using a hell of a lot of fuel — later I found out that 508 litres had been added to the 700 litres already on board before leaving the airport, and all of that, plus more, was needed.

As the chopper leaves, Chip changes the IV in my left arm from antinausea medication to the first bag of what is to total six litres of saline and Hartmans solution (electrolyte/dextrose). Its purpose is to raise my blood pressure and give my kidneys a chance when the pressure of the rock is released. Under instructions I hold the bag up with my right hand, alternating between raising it above the entry point and squeezing it under my arm. I must be beginning to slip in and out of consciousness now, as I'm starting to fall asleep, lowering the bag.

'Keep the pressure on that bag, Warren. Otherwise it could start to run backwards and you'll be losing fluid.'

I've begun to relax due to the combination of morphine and the total relief of not having to stay awake any more.

In a bit of a haze now, I'm greeted by Dany and Bill, complete with all the gear to get me out. They quickly introduce themselves, then quiz me on what exactly happened. They then begin preparing their gear, assessing the rock and how it's positioned on me. I explain how, because it's broken into two pieces, the weight is spread over both my legs, requiring the rock to be lifted straight up and not just on the one side.

Once Chip gets me stabilised, he pulls out a video camera. 'Do you mind if we film this, Warren? We do this sometimes to help us back up funding requests. At times, the government gets a bit tight fisted with the funding for equipment, and we find it helpful to have evidence of where their money has been spent — demonstrating how it has been used for specific rescues.'

I've got no problem with that. 'No worries mate. Are you going to use it on one of those rescue shows?'

'No, not quite. We use rescue videos in training to demonstrate the use of a particular piece of equipment also.'

Though I haven't really got any doubts, I'm hoping like hell these guys know what they're doing with this gear because, in a way, I'm not looking forward to this rock being lifted at all. *What if it falls again? I don't think I could handle that. But, then again, what else can I do?* I am fully aware that, if the rock falls, I will just want to die — if it doesn't kill me anyway.

It's not that easy, though, is it? What are you going to do — just hold your breath?

With my blood pressure steady at a much healthier 110 systolic now, Dany and Bill are ready to begin lifting the rock. Chip gives me a shot of adrenaline, knowing this to be a critical point in the operation. All the toxins, plus the potassium that has built up in my legs, will be released back into the blood stream as soon as the pressure is released. The adrenaline will help to keep my heart beating throughout.

With the jack positioned under the opposite side from me, between my feet, Bill begins slowly pumping the handle up and down, while Dany uses the crowbar at the broken edge to my left. Very carefully, they begin raising the rock, inching it higher before pausing to place a wooden chock underneath. It's not long before most of the weight is transferred to my left leg.

'Jesus, that hurts' is all I can manage in response to the pain.

With the bulk of the weight settling back onto the wooden chock, Bill moves the jack over to the right, changing over the contact plate, then setting it into its next position before beginning again. From side to side they work, with me drifting in and out of consciousness along the way a number of times. Chip tells me later that he was sure he was going to lose me at this point but I somehow managed to come back. All I feel is a huge sense of relief at being able to go to sleep while they work. No light at the end of a tunnel or anything like that. If this is dying, it doesn't seem any different from falling asleep. It is actually quite peaceful, and I'm no longer afraid of dying, from a pain point of view.

With the rock poised about ten centimetres above me now, we make the first attempt to get me out. We quickly encounter the problem that would have made it so difficult, even if Geert and I had been able to lift the rock, to actually get me out from underneath it. I'm lying back against a ridge of raised rock, with tree roots embedded in a crack running its length. This means I need to have enough clearance above my legs to allow my bum to be lifted up and over the rock and roots. So the guys continue lifting and jacking until the rock is about twenty centimetres above my legs, looming precariously over me. I'm desperately trying not to think about the consequences of it falling now. *No, it can't happen.*

'OK, are we ready to go?' Dany calls, standing behind me. As he supports me under the arms and lifts me, Bill keeps an eye on the jack and blocks while Chip looks after the lines trailing from me.

I'm pushing with all my might to get out from under there, which astounds Chip. He's just watched me return from the dead.

FREEDOM

'Get the hell off me!'

The enormous sense of freedom engulfs me. I can't move my legs at all, but the feeling attained from pushing out from under there is overwhelming. Even if I didn't actually do much, I think it was more the symbolic act in itself, the act of finally pushing the weight off me after all that time.

I'm loaded straight into a stretcher and covered with a space blanket before being strapped up in preparation for the winching into the chopper. The chopper has just returned, Chip signals it before realising it's not ours. It's the paparazzi, complete with bright spotlights and the obligatory cameraman hanging out the side. Chip gives them the 'fuck off' wave and, within a few minutes, they're replaced with the real thing.

It's all too clear to me how dangerous this is. If the stretcher starts to spin during winching, it can easily get out of control. Cutting the winch line can sometimes be the only action available to protect the chopper. Riding up with me is Chip, torch clenched between his teeth, beam flashing wildly across the scene below. Dany's below holding a stabilising line. It's almost completely dark now, a few minutes later and they would have had to abort the rescue, leaving Chip with me for the night. He's glad that didn't happen as he's got no doubt that I wouldn't have lasted the night. I'm glad I never had to find out.

Inside the chopper is almost as noisy as outside. I don't notice it for long, though. I slip into unconsciousness before Dany and Bill are winched up with all their tools.

Chip has got me rigged up to a monitor as the pilot, Tim Kesteven, lifts us out of the gully, turning towards Cairns Base Hospital. We cross the island in a couple of minutes, over the Hinchinbrook Channel, then on to Tully for a final refuelling. We arrive at the hospital at 8.39pm on Friday, April 11th 1997.

THE HOSPITAL

I wake to the feeling of being lifted, and open my eyes to see that I'm surrounded by people in white. I didn't even realise we'd landed. I feel like I'm on the roof of the hospital for some reason. When I see the helipad for the first time three weeks later, it doesn't look familiar at all. I'm transferred to a trolley, then wheeled in to the hospital. It all seems so dramatic. It doesn't really occur to me that I'm still in a pretty serious state. I'm floating on a sea of morphine, and still overcome with relief at having actually been rescued. I can feel myself moving but can't make out any features outside of my own space — just the sensation of moving forward, almost like I'm flowing through a mist.

Then I'm back again, this time in what looks like some kind of operating theatre. More faces looking down at me. Are they the same ones? I can't tell. I'm so tired, I just want to sleep. It's almost like I'm feeling the pain not so much as actual pain, but as a heaviness caused by the energy being drained from me. People are asking me questions, others monitoring equipment I am wired up to.

'What's your name?'

'Where do you live?' and so on ...

A woman introduces herself as Katherine Swanson, an orthopaedic registrar. 'We're going to have to let someone know what's happened to you, Warren. Is there anyone you'd like us to call?' she asks.

'Yeah, Dad would be best. I don't want to freak Mum out,' I reply through the oxygen mask.

'OK, what's his name and phone number?'

I give her Dad's details.

'Now, would you like me to call him for you?'

'No. It's OK. I can do it,' I reply.

'Are you sure? It might be better if I do it for you.'

'Yeah,' I'm nodding, eyes closed, realising how hard this is going to be, unsure of how I'm going to get the words out once I hear Dad's voice. A voice I hadn't expected to ever hear again only a few hours ago. Thinking about it later, I'm amazed she even gave me the option of calling myself.

She disappears from my side, only to be replaced by a man this time. He introduces himself, but his name, like many of the others, goes straight over the top of my head. 'Now, I'm going to touch you Warren. I want you to tell me when you feel anything, and where it is that you're feeling it.'

'OK.'

I'm looking up at the ceiling when he asks me the first time, 'Can you feel that Warren?'

I hesitate, not feeling anything. 'No,' I reply softly.

'What about this?' as he runs his finger higher up my leg.

'No. No. No. Maybe?' as he continues. *Did I feel something then or was it just my imagination?*

I look down as his fingers reach my penis. I hadn't noticed until now: it's swollen and twisted around like a corkscrew. I cringe at the sight of it, a lump in my throat as he asks me, 'What about this, can you feel anything now?'

'Yeah, sort of,' I answer hesitantly, knowing full well that I didn't feel a thing, but I had to give myself the benefit of the doubt. I refuse to even contemplate life without it, can't imagine how it would be worth going on.

I'm not giving anybody the green light to do anything hasty.

In retrospect, that decision could have made things a lot more complicated for me, but I suppose that was a chance I had to take. Given the situation again, I'd do the same thing.

'Now, Warren, this is going to be pretty uncomfortable mate, but we need to make sure your urethra hasn't been damaged. I'm going to have to insert this into your penis.'

He's holding up a length of plastic tubing with a bulbous end. It looks like it's going to be more than uncomfortable. 'OK,' I reply. On the one hand, I wish they'd just leave me alone to go to sleep. But on the other, I feel like the owner of a damaged car, just eager to see it fixed so I can drive it again, carry on my merry way.

Wincing as he inserts the plastic intruder, I don't realise that the very fact that it feels so uncomfortable is a good sign. I do have feeling there. Just.

'OK Warren, that's fine.'

Thank Christ for that.

I'm glad I can't see my legs clearly at this stage. The right knee looks smashed and swollen; same with my left ankle. What I don't notice was that they've turned blue, that the skin has begun to slough off in sheets.

Another guy moves to my side, introducing himself in a voice so soft that I'm straining to hear him. 'My name is Bill Clark, Warren. I'm a surgeon.'

With absolute compassion, he explains the situation to me quietly.

'Your legs have been very badly damaged Warren. The circulation has been cut off for almost forty-eight hours. The tissue has died. I'm afraid we can't save them.'

Squeezing my eyes shut tightly, I try to comprehend what he's saying, what I'd been shutting out since seeing the green spots on my foot.

It's true, this is really happening.

'I'm sorry, Warren, but we're going to have to amputate both your legs.'

My stomach knots, pulling my diaphragm up hard, forcing out a sniffling gasp as hot tears squeeze from my tightly closed eyes. My throat's so tight, I barely manage to get out:

'Both of them?'

'Yes, both of them. I'm sorry, Warren.'

So, it's true. I'd thought while I lay trapped that I might lose the foot I could see, the foot covered in green blotches. But I hadn't really let my mind dwell on the consequences.

Both of them. Both my legs!

Tears stream down my face. Not because I am thinking of what it will mean physically, how it will handicap me, turn me into a cripple. But through the sheer loss. I can't imagine them not being there. My toes, my feet, my legs have been there my whole life. The sheer loss, of losing part of myself, tears at me like the pain of losing someone you love.

Struggling to get my words out, not knowing whether I want to hear an answer: 'How high?'

'Fairly high, Warren. Above your knees.'

No! Fuck! I cry out inside, my body shivering deep inside. 'When?'

'We need to operate as soon as possible, tonight,' his reply.

No! Jeeeeeesus Christ!

'Is there anything else you can do? Can't you wait to see if they get any better?'

'If we wait, Warren, for some kind of improvement, I'm afraid I don't think you will survive the night. Of course, we need your permission to carry out the operation. But it's my personal and professional opinion that if we don't carry out the operation tonight, there's a very high chance you won't survive the night.'

My head feels like it's being squeezed from all sides, the pressure trying to compress my brain. I feel like I'm bracing myself for what I have to say.

'All right. Just do what you have to do.'

The words draining me completely, as if part of my spirit has gone with them. I sign the permission form for the operation with tears running down my face.

Lying there naked under all those lights, I begin to retreat into myself. Searching for strength. Crying. Feeling a sadness like I've never felt before. I can't begin to imagine the realm into which I'm heading, to comprehend what lies in front of me. I've never even had an operation before. I can't imagine my legs being cut.

Will it hurt? Will I die?

The magnitude of the situation overwhelms me.

I'm totally closed off from everything happening around me now, like I'm in some kind of tunnel, or a room full of mirrors. Everything else is irrelevant as I cry myself to sleep, knowing I'm embarking on a journey into total darkness. And that, if I do come out, things can never be the same again.

By 2.30am on Saturday morning, both my legs had been amputated at mid-thigh.

GEERT VAN KEULEN: **Friday morning, April 11th**

After a horrible night (I can't remember much of it but do know it was a bad trip), I packed my gear for the last time. A few droplets of a small shower fell on the tent. It was very overcast and cold. I managed to put some muesli in my mouth but was stiff and sore all over my body. At 5.30am I washed myself in the ocean, dressed and had a snack. Slowly I packed my rucksack with stiff and sore fingers, swung it over my shoulders and started my struggle towards the jetty, starting point of the trek. I knew that I should be able to make it to the jetty in three or four hours, hoping to catch the first tourist boat of the day. It was sheer agony but I finally got there just before 10.00am.

There were two trekkers there. Two bushwalkers from Queensland who had walked the trek from the opposite direction and were waiting for the boat to take them back to Cardwell. When I saw them on the far end of a sandy clearing in the mangroves I waved and noticed that most of my voice had disappeared. I remember thinking and fearing that they wouldn't believe my desperate need for help! After all, my story must have sounded pretty unbelievable.

In staccato and with a lot of difficulty I explained to them what had happened. My tongue seemed to have lost its function. It was glued to my palate. Words came out very slowly. I was very thirsty and asked for water; one of the guys gave me his water bottle. Water had never tasted better. Then one of them went to the beach with me and we started to collect firewood, paper and plastic that had been washed ashore so we could build a fire, creating thick, black smoke. With a long stick he drew a message in the smooth layer of sand: 'SOS. MAN TRAPPED UNDER ROCK FOR 36 HOURS' — letters about one metre in size — once again trying all we could to attract a plane.

One of the guys stayed at the jetty to warn as soon as a boat came in. They expected a boat at noon but at noon there arrived no boat. Once again my patience was tested and I spent the time sitting or lying on the beach. Trying to sleep or trying to spot Warren's position on Mount Bowen. To me all the beauty of the mountain had disappeared. Lying on the paradisiacal beach, I looked up. The weather had improved a great deal and there was sunshine all around me. Except for above the mountains on the island. How weird!

The two Aussies had run out of water themselves and I decided to stroll back down the long beach of Ramsay Bay to find a freshwater stream where I could drink and fill the water bottles. It was a fair walk and I was a little annoyed that neither of the two other walkers offered to get some water for me. One of them just hung around on the jetty while the other one was much more active and aware of the precarious situation of both Warren and myself. But I didn't feel like arguing, and went. I filled my bottle, emptied it in my mouth, refilled both and strolled back.

The walk to the stream was hard, even without the pack, and close to the stream I trod on a cane toad. It scared me; for an instant I thought I would break up. Then I wandered back to my waiting post again, not knowing when or if a boat would come in. It was well possible that it wouldn't because the bad weather kept the boats wisely ashore. Maybe no more tourists would arrive today? But the others had booked their trip in advance so one should come.

Half an hour before I left Warren he had told me that he could hold out one more night but not a second. If a rescue party could not get him out before nightfall the next day, he was sure he was going to die. The calm composure with which he told me this made such an impact on me that I could not doubt his own feelings. I was sure he had an immaculate sense of timing and understanding of his own strengths.

Later in hospital he told me that he knew that if I had gotten him out from underneath the rock after the long hours of work, he would have had a big chance of dying. The acid builds up in the blood after it has been cut off for such a long time and it could have poisoned him! He would certainly have had thrombosis. But he had to get out as the water rose, and his pain and sense of complete helplessness was much stronger than being able to do nothing and wait. Walking back to the area near the fire and the message, I thought about his words.

SOS

When I was approaching the area where I had rested I saw one of the bush-walkers waving to me. I managed to walk a bit faster and hurry towards a very serious and helpful boatman. They'd explained the situation and the man was busy off-loading his tourists, after which he took me on his boat. The man's name tag said 'Goody' — his nickname, I guess — and good he was. Goody sped back into the mangrove channels and found his way to the open sea. He was very professional about it. Didn't doubt my words for a moment and went straight into action. I must have looked a bit like a scarecrow, I realised later.

The open sea was the only place where Goody could put out a Mayday, but, alas, his radio could still not transmit. Our very beautiful Hinchinbrook Island and its Mount Bowen were in the way! But he remembered that there were a few crab boats sheltering somewhere in the mangrove channels and started looking for them. Finally, after sailing through the channels for maybe half an hour, he found one. An old Hemingway-ish character, a 'crabby', came on deck when he spotted us and helped to pull us on board. He looked like he'd walked off the set of an old movie: short, elephant skin, unshaven, grey-haired and tough as a nail. We shook hands with him and he got out his own mobile telephone and tried to get contact. After trying several times for about fifteen minutes he managed to contact the Hinchinbrook Resort, a Barrier Reef resort on another island nearby.

I had written a list with information about where Warren was, what time it had happened, his spirits and injuries; and Goody slowly repeated the words to the operator on the resort. When this was done we sailed back to the jetty, leaving Hemingway behind with his love of his solitary life.

I thanked Goody for his help. This man had acted as an important part in the chain of Warren's rescue. He took the two Aussies and two day-trippers back on board and left me behind on the beach. It was 2.30pm and there I sat once more — waiting, impatient. On the same spot in the sand. New threatening dark clouds gathered above Bowen. I smoked a rollie and lay down, my head resting on my pack. The pack was very damaged — straps were broken, plastic joints too, and the bottom part was ripped. My boots also were ripped on both sides. The pack had been on my back at a high altitude in Nepal and it had accompanied me on what also was a hairy adventure in the Pyrenees mountains in Spain. I felt very attached to it and I vowed never to throw away either the pack or the boots. I was sure my girlfriend would understand this time.

Three thirty. No helicopter yet. Where the hell are they? Time is really running out now. The SOS message was passed on nearly two hours ago. I'm uncertain of myself and impatient. 'Is Warren still alive? Is the chopper coming? Can I join them? Do I have to camp another night out here?' I tell myself to calm down and that the waiting will end soon.

Sometimes I dozed off but the adrenaline was still pumping too hard for me to sleep. Kept scanning the air. East, west and south from me,

I expected a green army chopper as both Townsville and Cairns have bases. Finally, at 4.30pm, I saw a very small black fly hovering against the dark background of Mount Bowen. It circled there for maybe ten minutes, then came my way. I got up with incredible joy. Took my sarong out of my pack and started waving and trying to yell.

Up there in the chopper they must have spotted me straight away, with their trained eyes, but I wasn't sure and made certain they couldn't avoid me. When it was a few hundred metres away it circled around and flew towards me over the sand dunes. The wind swept me nearly into the Barrier Reef!

The chopper landed on the beach and two people got out. One was crew, the other a policeman from Cardwell, dressed in a blue overall. He had guided the QES helicopter towards me. They both ran towards me and in my excitement I threw my pack over my shoulders and made attempts to run towards them. But the crewman waved a determined 'No' to send me back. I lost it a bit, I guess, being in some kind of shock.

The policeman walked away from me and sat down in the grass on the edge of the beach. The crewman, whose name was Greg Beer, put both his arms firmly around me and told me to bend my head. We ran to the chopper. Or rather, he dragged me to the chopper while the wind from the rotors blew the fine sand in our faces. He guided me carefully but very firmly into the co-pilot's seat, then put a headset on my messy curls. Just before getting on board himself, he explained how I could communicate with the other members aboard.

I looked over my shoulder and saw four very serious looking men looking at me from the back section of the helicopter. All were dressed in black over-alls and wearing helmets with big black visors, and were strapped into the harnesses that had to guide them down. Sweat ran in straight lines down their faces. The crew was very concentrated and ready to do whatever it took to get Warren out. I looked at the pilot who nodded in a friendly way to me. A little button on the floor near my right foot had to be pushed so I could hear the others and was able to communicate with the crew. As soon as I'd worked it out the doctor asked me about Warren's situation.

'How was he when you left him behind? How were his spirits?'

'Good when I left him,' I answered.

All kind of figures and numbers went up in the ether and the rotors started to rev up. Sand blew around the helicopter, the noise came to a high pitch and we were in the air. Crewman Dany, a strong, bearded Frenchman who'd grown up in Australia, showed me a crowbar and asked if they were able to get him out with that tool. I shook No, and supported my action by words while stepping on the floor button. The pilot asked me how to get to the accident site and I told him to follow the beach to the lagoon behind Little Ramsay Bay.

'Fly to the lagoon, follow the creek upwards, he should be a few hundred metres from a large cliff face,' I told him. We flew very quickly over the headlands I'd crossed earlier and in about ten to fifteen minutes were in the area, circling with the chopper's right side towards the mountain. All men looked with deep concentration into the green jungle below and suddenly I heard Dany call, 'I see him, he is waving his arm'!

He's alive!

Dany said more things but I have forgotten them. Forgotten because I became quite emotional. Tears came in my eyes and I smiled and laughed. Finally my emotions got a chance of coming out.

After that the chopper hovered around the site a bit. The crew probably took coordinates or established the exact location of Warren. The chopper turned around and made its way again to Ramsay Bay. I decided to enjoy the ride back to the beach.

The copper, called Ian, was still waiting in the grass bordering the sand dunes. He said that he experienced this quite regularly. With a need to impress me he began to tell me his tales but I soon stopped listening. Looking at the sea I felt tired, and within my own thoughts I stared away. After about ten minutes another helicopter that I never heard coming appeared in front of us. It landed only a small distance from us and out came a cameraman, a reporter and later the pilot of what was a chartered helicopter. Chartered by Channel Nine news.

'You're joking!' I thought and before I knew it the reporter started, quite diplomatically, to interview Ian. Then the reporter asked permission to interview me as well. I had no problems with that; in my mind Warren was alive and safe and I was overjoyed, so I let them ask their questions which I answered happily. I also walked a hundred yards or so over the beach while they filmed me with the island and Bowen in particular in the background. But I regretted it later. It felt weird to say the least. The chopper then waited for the rescue helicopter to return, meanwhile filming as much as possible.

The chopper was parked a few hundred metres away from me. It wasn't black or green but bright red, white and blue. Its rotor blades were bending down, slightly moving in the sea breeze. The crew seemed to work out a plan before they were going back to the accident site. I wondered what Warren would be thinking of. First he saw the chopper hovering in search for him, and then it left to return with me on board some fifteen minutes later. And it left once more to refuel on the mainland. Finally to return once more to drop off a few people. 'Would he have thought that they couldn't find him?' I wondered. It must have been a fantastic moment for him when he heard, then saw, the helicopter come around the mountain for the first time.

After half an hour the rescuers went back to the accident site to start their long fight against the clock, the weather and the darkness. My work was done.

The TV people filmed some of the operation from the air and then returned to Ian and me. They offered us a lift back to Cardwell, and we flew over the beach and filmed the message that had been drawn in the sand earlier in the day. Flying over Hinchinbrook Island, with the sun slowly setting, gave us quite majestic views. Knowing that Warren was being taken care of allowed me to enjoy the beauty of the place once more. From my seat in the back I could see Mount Bowen, then we flew over the mangrove forests and via the breathtaking Hinchinbrook Channel back to the coast.

While the crew chatted and discussed where they were going to spend the night it struck me that it was only routine for them. I thought about Warren and my friend in Townsville, Rohan. I longed for some friendship and felt the need to talk about the whole thing with someone I could trust. I was sure Rohan and Trish would fulfil that need.

The chopper landed on the football ground, from where a police car took me to Cardwell police station. I asked if I could take a shower at Ian's home, which he had told me was next-door to the cop shop. Free of the sweat and filth of my body, I waited back at the station to be taken to Townsville. I expected that a police report was going to be made of the events. It never happened. I chatted with Ian, who had dropped his macho façade, and to his assistant, beginning to relax a little. A local reporter connected to the Townsville *Bulletin* interviewed me and took a few photographs of me in front of a map of Hinchinbrook Island.

Minutes later my senses were on full alert once more, as a person walked in and announced that he was from the Marine Authority. When he started asking questions in a very authoritative and unfriendly way I realised that I had to be cautious. My suspicion was proved when he kept on asking to see my permit. 'Who gave you the permit?' he kept asking and I told him I couldn't remember. I thought I had lost it perhaps up on the mountain or maybe it was still somewhere in my pack. I certainly didn't feel like checking my pack for his sake. Had he been a little more tactful, I probably would have put in more effort to be of assistance to him.

Meanwhile I had developed a serious headache and when he kept on nagging I snarled: 'Look mate, I've just tried to save someone's life, am I in trouble or something?'

He backed off and the copper quickly stepped in and said that if he was ever going to go hiking he would ask me to join his party. Meanwhile the reporter had made a deal with the newspaper in Townsville. The policemen took me in their car to Ingham, halfway between Cardwell and Townsville, together with the films that had been taken. There I was to travel back to Townsville with another reporter from the newspaper. I picked up my back-pack, threw it in the back of the cop car and sat behind the plastic screen in the back seat, wondering what kind of people had sat in the same seat and in what condition! Ian and his mate chatted as I looked into the dark tropical night. Round about 8.00pm the radio crackled and someone in the chopper explained that Warren was in a 'stable condition' on his way to the hospital in Cairns. I felt happy.

At the police station in Ingham the films and I were transferred to another car which took me to Rohan's place.

'Make sure to drop by after a few days' rest,' the reporter said. 'We would like to report on your reunion with Warren and can organise transportation for you to go up to Cairns.'

'Maybe,' I said and was soon knocking on Rohan's door.

I had frightened Rohan and Trish when I called them from Cardwell police station, but now they realised what I had endured and they took care of me. We drank a little wine and scotch, chatted for some time (I can't recall about what) and listened to some relaxing jazz until quite late.

Saturday, April 12th

The next morning at the newsagency I discovered my ragged face on the cover of Rupert's newspaper.

'Desperate hike saves companion' the headline read, and I smiled and bought five copies to mail home. After I had read the article I called the hospital and after explaining who I was the nurse told me that I could talk to Warren directly by mobile phone! That's what we should have had up there. A mobile! Just about every Australian seemed to walk around with one.

I spoke to Warren, who was very doped up but managed to thank me and calmly told me that he had lost both of his legs. I couldn't believe it and asked him to repeat the words, which he did. I felt sad, through and through, and very angry. Never in my imagination did I envisage Warren without legs. But of course it made sense after the circulation had been cut off for such a long time. He had been trapped for forty-six hours.

The news shocked me. I felt like someone who has lost a dear friend or relative and can't believe that the person is gone. In anger I ran from Rohan's room and cried. I felt responsible and guilty for the accident as it was I who had asked him to come along with me. Rohan calmed me down and tried to talk some sense into me. I decided to go and visit Warren after the weekend.

At 6.00pm on the Saturday evening, WIN television network broadcast the story. It was the main news item, before the politics of Pauline Hanson and other news. It showed the accident site from the air, the rescuers working on Warren with tools and equipment, and the interview with me on the beach. Rohan videotaped the news and much later, when I was back in the safety of my own living room in the Netherlands, watching it helped me a great deal to overcome my trauma and to remember vital moments and scenery of the period I had spent on the island.

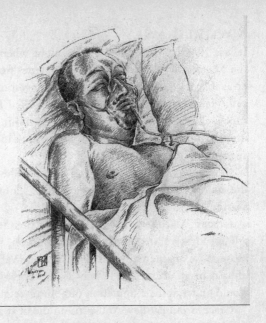

PART 2 THE WILL TO LIVE

'You are a child of the universe, no less than the trees and the stars ... With all its sham, drudgery and broken dreams, it is still a beautiful world.'

Desiderata

A WORLD AWAY

It was 10.00pm on a quiet Friday night when the telephone rang in the Macdonald household, 3500 kilometres from Cairns, in the western suburbs of Melbourne. Lisa, the youngest of four siblings, took the call. Her heart sank as the caller identified herself. Numbed with shock, she went back into the lounge room. Her mother, Patricia, immediately sensed something terrible had happened, crying in anguish, 'Who is it love?'

'It's someone from the Cairns hospital. She wants to talk to Dad,' she managed to utter, before bawling, 'Something's happened to Warren!'

Graeme Macdonald picked up the kitchen telephone, bracing himself for the worst. Dr Katherine Swanson, from the Cairns Base Hospital, explained to him that his son Warren had been gravely injured in an accident. He was about to go into surgery where he would undergo the amputation of both his legs.

Graeme and Pat flew to Cairns on the next available flight, arriving at the hospital at 11.15am on Saturday morning. After being briefed by a social worker, they met with Dr John Morgan, an intensive care specialist based at the Royal Brisbane Hospital, who was in Cairns on a locum. He explained the seriousness of their son's condition.

'We *think* that he'll make it,' he said gravely. 'But there is a chance he may die.'

Thirty minutes later, they would walk into the realm of their eldest son's new life.

SATURDAY MORNING

Almost like being suddenly grabbed and pulled up hard from beneath a murky sea, I wake feeling like I've had a torch shoved in my face in the middle of the night. Terror grips me as I realise I'm choking. I try to cry out but I can't.

Something's caught in my throat! I can't breathe!

I try to lift my arms but they move in slow motion, as if they are still under the water.

What the hell's down my throat? It's choking me!

'Get this thing out of my throat! I can't breathe! Somebody help me!' I plead, but nothing more than a groan escapes my chest.

My sudden movement attracts the attention of a nurse and she's quickly beside me, trying to reassure me. 'It's OK. You're all right. The tube is there to help you breathe. Just try to relax.'

'It's choking me! It's fucking-well choking me! Get it out! Please!'

Holding my arm, she keeps telling me I'm OK, but I try to struggle, my eyes widening, pleading for her to help me.

'Take it out, please! It's choking me!' I groan desperately.

Tears run down my face as I retch involuntarily, gagging on the plastic tube in my throat. Called an ET (for endotracheal) tube, it's pushed right down into my trachea, to the point before the branches to my right and left lung. Minutes pass. I'm still struggling, but I sense I can't take this thing out of my mouth, that it's there for a reason. As I slowly gain control over my throat convulsing, the discomfort is replaced with the pain that had lurked in the background for those first moments of my new life.

I feel like I've been hit by a truck, my whole body racked with a heavy, dull ache. Every bit of me is sore and tight. I am sure that I'm going to burst out of my skin. There's no additional pain in my legs, they're just as sore as everything else. Actually, I'm not really thinking about them. I remember what happened, the events of the previous days rushing into my thoughts like a train slamming into the station of my mind. I know my legs are gone. A deep sadness weighs heavily in my heart. Right at this moment, though, that was not my major concern. Overriding all else was one thought:

I am surely going to die.

The thought chills me inside, my stomach tightening, my entire body tensed as my breathing quickens in response to the realisation. I can't believe I've come all this way for this. Gone through everything I have, for it to end like this. The nurse is still beside me, reassuring me.

'It's OK. You're going to be OK. Just try to relax.' As she speaks, her attention is focused on a monitor behind me. Occasionally glancing down, making sure I haven't pulled out any of the multitude of lines and wires attached to me. An immeasurable period of time passes. I'm amazed that she is the only one here, that there aren't more people here to save me. When I have finally reached a point resembling 'relaxed', she leans over and says, 'There are some people here to see you.'

MUM AND DAD

Looking across the room, I see Mum and Dad moving towards me.

'Mum!' I whimper, unable to call out.

Reaching out, I take her hand and squeeze it tightly, the tears streaming down both our faces.

'Oh, love,' she manages to get out before closing her eyes in pain.

'Dad!'

Taking my other hand, 'We're here mate, it's all right,' he says, voice breaking as the tears run down his face. I close my eyes, sobbing with relief that I'm no longer alone.

Mum, barely able to speak, squeezes my hand tighter and says, 'I love you so much. You know that, don't you?'

I squeeze my eyes tight over burning tears and nod my head. *Yes, I do. I love you, too Mum.*

I become distressed at being unable to speak, the frustration adding to my woes. I need to talk to them, to let them know how heartening it is to see them. I wish more than anything else they could just take this tube out so I could talk to them, rather than have me slip away like this in silence. Waves of despair flood over me, threatening to drown me.

Nooooooo! Don't let it happen like this! I need to . . . write. That's it.

I motion for a pen, eyes pleading for recognition. I feel a sense of urgency, as if I could go this very minute, and it makes me frantic in my actions. Dad recognises immediately what I need and calls for the nurse, who reappears quickly with pen and paper. I have trouble holding the pen, my hands feeling like they are inside thick gloves. I can hardly put it to the paper. When I finally do, all that results is scribble. Mum and Dad are trying to read it as I look on in utter frustration. I motion for it back again, trying to take my time, but it still comes out just a scribbled mess.

Nooooooo! I scream inside with frustration.

One more try. Dad passes me the pad again and I slowly put the words together, using all my energy just to get them on the page:

Good to see you

'It's good to see you, too, love,' Mum cries, Dad squeezing my hand.

Having them there has begun to lift me, and I feel like I have to fight back. I motion for the pad and pen, and Dad passes it back to me. With determination I write:

No fucking rock is going to beat me

They both cry as they read it. I hold Mum's hand as I cry, too, face screwed up in anguish, hot tears squeezing from my eyes. It feels like this is the last time I'll ever see them, that we're saying goodbye. Utter devastation crashes down on me as I realise this could be my last chance to let them both know how I really feel. What I have never said. What most of us have probably never said.

Then I remember. *My red book! They've got to read my journal!*

Dad passes me the pad again, sensing my urgency. Slowly and deliberately, I write:

Red book

Dad reads aloud, 'Red book', looking to me for confirmation. I nod, squeezing my eyes shut with relief.

'Where is it mate?' he asks, and for a second I feel lost again.

I motion for the pad again and write, painfully slowly:

Plastic bag

I don't really know where it is. They might not even have brought it out with me. One of the rescue crew asked me, as they lifted me into the stretcher before flying out of Warrawilla Creek, whether any of my belongings were family heirlooms.

'If you don't absolutely need it, we're going to have to leave it here,' he said. My diary may have been left behind, washed down the creek by now. They may never get to read it.

'It's OK, mate. We'll find it,' Dad reassures me. I try to form words, but again they just come out in a groan, as I try to emphasise the importance of finding that book. I feel myself slipping off, my energy drained from the sheer emotion.

They've got to read it! is all that fills my mind as I drift off into an unknown time and space.

I can only now, in hindsight, begin to imagine what they must have been going through to see me like that. Their eldest son horribly disfigured, barely alive.

AWAKENING

The next time I wake, it must be late at night. It's very quiet and at first I think I'm alone. The tube is gone from my throat! The relief sweeps over me that I'm not choking any more. All I can think about is how thirsty I am; my throat feels so dry, it's like cardboard. I still can't think about what's happened. My mind is being occupied by other things, like thirst and pain. Seemingly from nowhere, a nurse appears at my side.

'How are you feeling?' she asks.

'OK, I think.'

'Can I get you anything?' she asks.

'I need something to drink, my throat's so dry,' I reply in a hoarse whisper.

'What would you like?'

'What have you got?' I asked.

'We've got some cold water, or some cordial.'

'Have you got anything fizzy?' I ask, thinking I might be asking a bit much.

'Yeah, I could probably find you something in the kitchen. What would you like?'

'A can of Coke?' I ask hopefully, surprising myself as soon as the words leave my lips. I don't usually drink Coke. Well, not unless it's mixed with bourbon!

'I think I may be able to dig something up for you,' she smiles, and leaves the room. I don't think I've ever anticipated a mere drink so much before. I haven't had any fluids pass my lips since Friday afternoon. It is now somewhere around 8.00pm, Saturday night. *I am so thirsty!*

The nurse returns with an icy cold can, popping a straw into it before handing it to me, still holding onto it to save me from spilling any. I suck at it greedily, almost too quickly, and she stops me from drinking too much. The feeling, as thousands of tiny bubbles explode over my tongue, is like heaven. With incredible satisfaction, totally refreshed, I close my eyes and drift back into the hazy realm of a deep, dreamless sleep.

I wish now I could remember what my mind could possibly have been dreaming at that time, hovering between life and death. However,

I draw a blank. Dosed up on a combination of Fentanyl, a powerful narcotic, and Midazolam, it's a wonder I remember anything at all. Midazolam is a sedative, similar in effect to Valium. A standard dose of 5 milligrams two to three times per day produces an amnesic effect. I am on 5 milligrams per hour!

I awake to find a number of people talking at the foot of my bed, one of whom introduces himself as Dr John Morgan.

'So, how are we feeling?' he asks.

'All right,' comes my reply.

'You're a lucky man. You must be a strong bugger to still be with us, you know.'

'I don't know about that,' I reply, not really feeling that lucky.

'Do you understand what's happened to you?' he asks seriously.

'Yeah, I think so,' I answer, hoping there is no more to know than the obvious.

'We have had to amputate both your legs,' he begins. 'They were very badly damaged and couldn't be saved.'

I nod in reply as my throat tightens at hearing it said for the first time. Nobody has mentioned my legs up until now. I still feel like I am fighting for my life, and haven't stopped to dwell on my legs.

'We have left the wounds open, Warren, so we can monitor them for a few days. Once we can be sure there's no infection, we'll close them up.'

'OK' was all I could say. *So it's not over, I've got to have another operation.*

Shuddering when I think about my legs now, trying to comprehend that they're gone, knowing that the wounds have not been closed, I picture the ends, open and bloody, flaps of skin draping over them. The thought turns my stomach. *Christ, I hope they close them up soon.*

Dr Morgan, finished with me now, briefs the nurse beside him before leaving. I go back to floating on my sea of obscurity, not aware of any pain now, just the bizarre feeling that my feet feel squashed. Like they've been squeezed into a pair of shoes that are much too small. And they're cold! Both my legs feel really cold and numb. Looking down my body to the empty space under the sheets, I consciously have to push the rising thoughts out of my head. *Don't, mate. Don't even think about it. Not yet.*

I drift off into the sanctuary of sleep, only to be awoken a short time later by the nurse. 'You've got some visitors. Would you like to see them?' she asks.

'Yeah, who is it?' I ask, looking towards the door as Mum and Dad walk in, my question answered.

'How are you, love?' asks Mum, holding my hand and leaning down to hug me gently. 'I'm all right,' I manage to get out, my eyes holding back tears. 'G'day Dad,' and I reach out my hand to take his.

'Did you find it?' I ask, my voice strained with emotion. 'Did you find my journal?'

'Yes, mate. We found it,' says Dad, squeezing my hand tighter.

'Did you read it?' The tears are threatening to squeeze out.

'We did, love,' Mum replies, leaning down to hug me again, eyes welling.

'That was the hardest thing I've ever had to do,' she cries. I hold her tight, trying to imagine how it must have been for her to read. Knowing that, as I wrote, I fully expected to die. That these were in fact my last words.

'I love you, Warren,' she sobs into my shoulder.

'I love you, too, Mum,' I cry, holding her tightly, hot tears streaming down my face. We hold each other for some time before Mum breaks the silence.

'There's someone else here to see you, love. Lisa flew up this morning. Would you like to see her?'

'Yeah, I would,' I reply, my joy also mixed with an uneasiness at her seeing me like this. I've always been her big brother. We have always been close, the youngest and the oldest, and I fear how she may perceive me now.

When she walks into the room and comes towards me, tears filling her eyes, I lose it again. Taking my hand and leaning down to me, she cries into my shoulder, 'I love you, Wogsy.'

'I love you too, Lee,' I sob as I hold her tight, choking with emotion. It is so good to see her. I haven't seen any of my family since flying down to Melbourne for Dirty and Sharon's wedding, back in February. Seeing Lisa again now, after what I have gone through, I feel as if I've been given a second chance.

ACCEPTANCE

I spent the next ten days in the intensive care ward. I feel now as if I was in some kind of hazy limbo, like time had swirled around me like a fog. At times, I felt no pain at all. At others, I ached all over, a deep ache that seemed to penetrate my bones. My skin still felt incredibly tight, stretched over my swollen body, squeezing me.

I felt completely drained, explained possibly by the fact I was losing almost two litres of blood per day during those first few days. The blood was being continuously replaced through my IV line, the nurse repeatedly changing the bags hanging on the stand beside me. During my stay in intensive care, I would receive a total of 15.15 litres, consisting of 35 units of packed cells (red blood cells) at 330ml per unit, 30 units of platelets (the clotting mechanism of blood) at 70ml per unit and 10 units of fresh frozen plasma at 150ml per unit. Considering that the average person has 6.5 litres of blood in their body, I had lost a hell of a lot!

Only a few days after the initial operation the nurses began bringing me a cordless telephone whenever someone called for me. At times talking to people gave me enormous strength. At others, when I couldn't see any way out, it just made me feel worse. During those times, I declined to talk, asking the nurses to tell the caller I was OK, or getting Mum or Dad to speak to them if it was someone they knew. Messages and cards offering best wishes and support came flooding in, and I was often moved to tears by friends putting feelings that are rarely expressed into words.

When the call came through from Geert, I took the telephone anxiously. Amazingly, I had almost forgotten about him, my thoughts occupied somewhat. But I needed to thank him. Wanted to hear his story and let him know I was OK.

He was calling from Townsville, staying with friends, trying to rest and take in what had happened. He told me how a television helicopter had given him a ride off the island. I reassured him that I was OK, that my family were with me now. I wasn't prepared for his next question, though.

'How are your legs, mate. Were they broken?' My stomach churned with the realisation. *He doesn't know!*

'Didn't they tell you?'

'Tell me what?' he asked, concern filling his voice.

I swallowed hard before answering, 'They had to cut them off mate.'

A stony silence filled the line, neither of us speaking for what seemed like an eternity.

'Christ, Warren. I don't know what to say,' he said finally, his voice a hollow shell for the words.

'It's all right, mate. You did everything you could.' My voice was strained. 'You got me out of there. You saved my life.'

A silence took over the line, the kind of silence that says more than words. 'Can I come up and see you Warren?'

'Yeah, mate. That'd be good.'

On Wednesday, the rest of my family flew up from Melbourne to see me. Michelle came in first. As we held each other, tears streaming down her face, I thought of how she must have felt. Michelle is a nurse; medically she must have known how bad it was from the start. She must have witnessed this scenario a hundred times from the relative comfort of the sidelines.

I went through the same apprehension with the rest of the family that I had gone through with Lisa, especially with Matty, my nephew. When my brother Brett walked into the room with him, Matthew looked anxiously at the place where my legs were supposed to be, then ducked down to see if he could see them hanging beneath the bed. He must have thought it was some kind of magic trick. The concept of someone having their legs cut off would be too strange for him to come to grips with. He kept his distance from me, almost as if he was too scared to get any closer. It was my first experience of the way kids respond when they see me now. I scare them, and it's a feeling I'll never get used to.

Seeing my family again totally drained me. Such intense emotions had been dragged to the surface, ranging from the pure joy of being alive with them, to the fear and doubt of their acceptance. A fear I can best explain now by recounting a scene in an African documentary I saw twelve months later.

The scene is set around a rapidly diminishing water hole, left behind after the river ceased to flow through the onset of the dry season. As the only source of water left in the area for all the animals, it becomes the focal point for their survival. However, through a cruel twist of fate, it is full of crocodiles. They're massed together in what becomes no more than a mud slurry, lying in wait for the next thirsty baboon or impala to take their chance and venture forward.

As the mud hole evaporates, reducing more and more, it becomes a seething pit of crocodiles. Writhing and rolling, they fight amongst themselves over the carcasses of the victims so far. Nothing but a few boggy holes, mainly hoof prints filled with water, remain near the edge. But still these are within the crocs' reach, and each animal that ventures forward to drink is dragged into the pit.

An atmosphere of madness begins to take hold, an insanity wrought from the absolute helplessness, the total cruelty of the whole situation. Like a scene set in hell, where there is no happy ending, only pro-longed pain and suffering. One by one, animals are drawn to the water through desperation, then quickly torn apart by the waiting crocs. There is no option but to drink; otherwise they will die of thirst.

Eventually, a young baboon ambles forward to the edge, desperate for water. Deciding, I suppose, that it is better to risk dying in the effort than slowly to die of thirst under the hot sun.

As he bends down to drink, a huge croc leaps forward, seizing the terrified baboon by the head. The baboon, squealing in terror, has both hands on the croc's jaws, trying to pry them open, to pull his head out of its vice-like jaws. For what seems like an agonising eternity, he's held there, on the bank, until, miraculously, he breaks free! Scampering back up the bank, bleeding from deep gashes to his head, he looks terrified. He stops at the top of the bank and looks frantically around with haunted eyes, needing some kind of support from someone. Some comfort.

All he is met with are stares. The other baboons look upon him as a ghost, as if he shouldn't be alive, not after that. They're scared of him, possibly scared of what he's been through. Why? Is it because it forces them to face their own mortality? Or that they don't know what to say to him — that this is too much to take on board, the emotional scar he will carry with him?

Why is it that we are scared of people who have been to the edge. Is it because they have had a glimpse of the other side, and we don't want to contemplate what they saw, opting instead for blissful ignorance?

Never have I felt so much pity for another being as I did for the baboon standing there alone, desperately needing someone to go to him, to hold him. Comfort him. But nobody came. He was no longer one of them.

THE SURGERY NEVER STOPS

During the ten days I spent in intensive care, I went into theatre a further five times. Most of the early operations involved the debridement of necrotic tissue, but one, carried out only four days after my initial surgery, resulted in my right femur being shortened a further four centimetres due to infection in the bone.

Dr Morgan was concerned about the smell coming from one of my stumps, the smell of rotting flesh. I didn't even notice it before he mentioned it, and I suppose nobody else was game to say anything. *'Gee, your legs stink!' I don't think so.* I was impressed to see a doctor using a skill as basic and down to earth as his sense of smell to evaluate the situation. When a patient's wounds smell like a bag of prawns left out in the sun all day, there's really no need to sit around and wait for lab results.

I dreaded the occasions on which Dr Morgan came to check on me, sniffing around my dressings. I knew that if it didn't smell good, I'd be off to the operating theatre again. The thought of further operations terrified me. Not just because of my fear of being cut open while I'm asleep — that alone is bad enough. But what scared me more was that, each time they operated, they would be taking another piece of me away.

Surely I can't lose any more of my legs! Haven't I lost enough already?

Each time the rotting smell raised its head again, I went into a deep depression, just praying for an end to this so I could start to recover. I felt like I wasn't actually getting anywhere. Like I was hanging in the balance, still capable of going either way. Each time I went into theatre, I came out so drained that I felt I was back to square one.

Time became meaningless as I went from recovering from one operation to being prepared for the next, seemingly with no breaks in between. Before each operation, the dreaded 'Nil by mouth' sign would be hung on the end of my bed. For eight hours prior, I was allowed no food or drink, to ensure an empty stomach in the operating theatre. The food part I didn't have a problem with. I had no appetite at that stage anyway. But the lack of fluid I found almost unbearable. I had been so thirsty ever since waking up in hospital, and just couldn't seem to get enough fluid into me. Not being able to drink almost sent me around the bend. I'd beg the nurses to at least give me one of their foul tasting, lollypop-like, lemon-glycerin swab sticks. Sucking them at least made you feel you were getting some fluid. I actually got to like them in the end, which was a bit of a worry!

I'd begun to feel like my life was on hold, as though it hung in the balance, waiting for someone to make a decision as to which way it would go. I couldn't think beyond the present, couldn't picture life beyond the room I was in. All I could focus on was getting better, and that depressed me more than anything because it was beyond my control. My legs were still plagued by infection, and I prayed each time I woke after theatre, or Dr Morgan entered the room on his ward round, that it was over. That there'd be no more surgery. That they had finally cut out all the infection and would now leave me alone. Only then could I regain control, be back in charge of my own destiny.

In the meantime all I could do for myself was to keep my sanity by totally blocking out what had happened to me. I was in no fit state to deal with that now. There would be plenty of time for that later.

Having two of my closest friends come up to Cairns to see me lifted my spirits enormously — just knowing they were there, realising that they cared enough to be with me when I needed them most. Belinda Wells flew all the way from Melbourne and Natalie Dudding, who is like a third sister to me, caught the train up from Brisbane. I can't imagine what it must have been like for them to see me as I was, but I am glad they had the courage to walk into that room. I only wish they could have both been there at the same time so they could finally meet, but they missed each other by a matter of days.

They, along with Mum and Dad, came in to see me every day of their respective visits, bringing me fresh juice and anything else I needed. Mum and Dad moved out of the motel they'd been staying in, invited by friends Paul and Karen Wilson to share their home. A Qantas pilot, Graham Bigby (known to Dad through his work as a maintenance specialist with Qantas), gave them the use of his car. They stayed with me for the whole month I spent in Cairns, for which I will be eternally grateful.

I felt guilty that I had spent so much time away from my family, wondering now whether it had been selfishness on my part. I hoped they could understand my need to follow what drove me on, the constant quest for adventure, the search for meaning. It was always so good to see them again after I'd been away for a while. They gave me a sense of stability. But before too long, I always found myself feeling anxious again — as if I was missing out on something by sitting back in comfortable surroundings rather than being out there, at the frontier.

Life is not something to be experienced from a lounge-room chair. I have always felt agitated if I'm not challenging myself in some way. I am not worth being around when I feel caught in a rut, and at those times I don't like to inflict myself on other people. I learnt, through having Mum and Dad up there with me, that they would always support me in whatever I did as long as I was happy.

My physiotherapist had given me an instrument she wanted me to use called a Triflow — a clear plastic gadget housing three hollow balls. I had to blow into it, trying to keep all three balls suspended as long as possible on a cushion of air. This was to keep my lungs active and prevent them from holding fluid. Apparently this is a big problem when a patient is immobilised for any length of time, and can cause them to contract pneumonia. I became obsessed with it, using it at every opportunity. I recognised it as the first active step. The first part for me to play in my own recovery.

GEERT VAN KEULEN: **Reunion**

On the Thursday after Warren was rescued I took the bus from Townsville to Cairns to visit him at the Cairns Base Hospital. No newspaper or film crew was going to hover around Warren. I made sure of that and ignored their offer of travelling with their support.

The days since returning from the island had been filled with relaxing, and trying to get the adrenaline level down (which just didn't happen). For days I could not sleep properly, nor unwind. The headaches got worse and some-times it seemed the whole side of my head ached. At Rohan and Trish's place I had found a perfect shelter. I called my girlfriend and parents and explained what happened. But I wanted to recuperate more before heading back home. When I felt ready I decided to visit Warren. I wasn't sure whether he would want to see me, or even whether he could, so I called the hospital first and spoke to a nurse who said it would be important for me to come down. So I boarded a bus in Townsville and headed for Cairns, a six-hour trip. Having checked in to a guesthouse, I threw my stuff in my room and went straight to the Cairns Base Hospital.

On arrival I was snatched by two social workers who knew about my visit. For about half an hour we talked about the accident and I was given a pile of articles on how to deal with trauma. 'Survivor guilt', they called the symptoms I was showing.

I sterilised my hands and was allowed on the intensive care ward, where I met one of Warren's sisters, Michelle. She cried a little and hugged me, then thanked me for what I'd done. I felt quite overwhelmed by it and uneasy.

Warren was in a mess of wires, computers, monitors and LED lights, heavily breathing through a mask and fighting it. He had just come out of theatre and was under a heavy dose of narcosis. Lots of morphine. I looked at him and where I expected his legs was a sheet and a white blanket. Half a human being! His thighs were slightly spread out and covered by a thick layer of bandages. His legs had been removed to about ten or fifteen centimetres above his knees, one left a bit longer than the other. Every few minutes a little alarm would go off and a nurse came by to change a drip or check on the equipment around him.

The social workers watched how I approached Warren, then left me with him. I stroked his forehead and looked at his face. His small beard, ginger coloured, was tightened to his face because of the mask. I looked around the room. The hospital was in an old building. In contrast with a lot of the surrounding buildings in Cairns this place was in financial need. The apparatus and equipment, however, seemed modern, as far as I could judge. The wall next to Warren was covered with yellow Post-It Notes carrying a load of well-wishing messages from friends all over Australia. A few postcards had already made it to the hospital too and I noticed that my address and telephone number in Townsville were pinned on the wall.

I whispered a few words to him and his eyes opened a little and slowly scanned the room. When they met mine he said, 'Thank you, mate. I didn't think you'd make it.' I suppose he meant the hike down the mountain, not the trip to the hospital. After that he fell silent. There wasn't much to talk about at this stage and I sat down on a stool by his bed. I felt relieved, tired and humble.

'Another job done,' I thought to myself, as I had really worked myself up to go here. I knew I had to, and there was no way I wouldn't have done it, but I felt very uneasy about it. Being confronted with his parents and other relatives was going to be another difficult part of the visit. But now, the tiredness manifested itself for the first time since the accident and I felt sleepy. The adrenaline had not stopped pumping until now. Incredible how much stress my head had to endure, even after the accident. I yawned, and smiled a little when I noticed myself.

Looking at Warren slowly coming out of the worst of the narcoses, his big, strong shoulders, chest and arms against the white bed linen, wires and tubes connected to them, I marvelled at his natural sense of humour and strong will to live, and found myself wondering 'What if this accident had happened to me . . . ?'

Noise in the corridor roused me up out of my daydream and his parents all of a sudden stood in front of me. His mother hugged me and cried and his dad said, 'How can I ever thank you?' To which I must have mumbled something, which I can't remember. I had imagined these people being very angry with me for taking Warren on the trek but instead I found respect and gratitude. Although it's very important that they treated me in that nice way, I did not feel like I deserved it. The guilt was too strong and I felt a great deal of sympathy for his parents. Difficult.

Later during my visit, three members from the QES rescue chopper crew walked in. Obviously, it wasn't the first time they had checked on Warren. They were the pilot, winchman and a crewman and it got quite crowded on intensive care. The winchman asked if I had built the back support which they found Warren in. I said yes and he explained that building the chair had actually saved Warren's life. Had he been lying down, his lungs would have not been able to cope and he would have died! By sitting upright this was avoided. I hadn't realised that it was so important. My aim had been to give him a little comfort. But it was nice of the crew member to point this out because it relaxed me a little. The crewmen also asked if I was all right. 'Yeah,' I replied and thanked them for their lifesaving work. One of them made a joke about my appearance at the beach; saying, 'Well, you finally had a shave!' to which Warren supplied, from beneath his oxygen mask, 'Yeah, he's a bit of a wild man. A wild man from Borneo!' After which he drifted away once more.

Round about 5.00pm I left Warren behind in his Star Wars room, together with the monitors, tubes and drips. There were more casualties on intensive care and I witnessed how a nurse on duty volunteered to be a blood donor on the ward. They drew blood from her in between the beds, so to speak.

I walked on the streets of Cairns. The Esplanade, where 14 years before I had walked with a Dutch friend and later with my partner to be, Annabel. 'The mud banks on the other side of the Esplanade will be here in another fourteen years' time and much longer,' I thought. 'At least that will be unchanged.'

Back at the hostel, the music was very loud — Bob Marley was telling a partying young audience to get up and stand up for their rights — so I put my waxy earplugs firmly in my ears and tried to sleep a little. Once again I couldn't relax. My head hurt badly. Too much was happening, still. I packed my gear and walked to a quieter hostel where I took a shower and managed to relax a little. When I arrived back at the hospital at 8.00pm, Warren was being transferred from intensive care to the coronary ward. This gave him more space and quietness as he was the only patient on the ward. A much better environment for him and not as stressful as being on intensive care.

There I met a charming friend of Warren's who'd come all the way from Brisbane by train (a 32-hour trip!) to stand by him — Natalie from New Zealand. The three of us chatted for a while. Warren was once again trying to be funny. I showed him the sketches of the accident that I had drawn from memory. But realised that I'd been premature in hoping we could talk about it. He had other things on his mind. I had made photocopies of the drawings, my notes and a few newspaper articles that I'd gathered and left these with him. I was sure one day he would or could use it.

At 10.00pm we two visitors left and walked into the warm tropical Cairns night. Over a drink, Natalie gave me a good opportunity to tell my story. The gratitude and support I received from her were also good to experience. At 11.00pm I hit the sack in my quiet hostel. I was plagued by my usual burning headache on the left-hand side of my head, starting at the top of my head, then travelling down to behind my eyes, to my teeth and disappearing below my shoulders. Fortunately, it couldn't prevent me from falling asleep a little while later.

The next morning I went back to the hospital at 11.00am and found Warren in the company of his parents and Natalie. He was happy to see me. I discovered a spark in his eyes that hadn't been there in the days before. Immediately after I'd first heard that he'd lost his legs, I wondered if he would want to live, being such a fit man suddenly becoming invalid. Now I was very happy that he still was. I think that there is a good future left for this strong individual.

After talking to him and his parents for a while, Natalie and I decided to go for a walk. We lunched at the art gallery, then sat down on a bench looking at the mudflats. I sketched the scene in front of me, and looked around, as we chatted. Together we went through the history of the past couple of days. Of course it had come to her as a shock, too, and she had no rest left inside her after she received the news and had to get the train up here.

She told me that Warren had been critically bad on the Tuesday, three days before, and his mother had also told me that even she had thought that Warren would not see the end of that day; his face was very swollen and his attitude was very lethargic. But from the next day things went up for him. Natalie told me about some of the peculiarities in his character and of his sense of humour. We discussed the use of meditation and rest, and quietly talked until it was time for another visit to the hospital. This time I saw Warren only for five minutes because he was very tired and needed all the rest he could find.

Natalie and I joined the Macdonald family for dinner that night and they let me feel that I was, for that occasion at least, one of them. A kind way of showing gratitude. At their encouragement, I ate an enormous sirloin steak, garnished with pepper sauce. It just about fitted on my plate. The Queensland way. I drank three glasses of South Australian Cooper's ale and found the evening comfortable and happy. Warren kept on coming up in the conversations and people were eager to listen to my side of the adventure too. The conversation never seemed to get a sad undertone. Everyone was very relieved and happy that Warren was still amongst us.

Saturday, April 19th

Diary: I'm sitting outside a coffee shop somewhere in Cairns. 'Mozart's' this place is called. It's fairly quiet at this time of the morning but every now and then the peace is disrupted when large buses drive by. Loaded with bungee jumpers, reef divers and snorkellers, paintballers and whitewater rafters. A lot of money is being circulated in this town. Japanese and Western. The laid back atmosphere from fourteen years ago has gone. Today is going to be my last day here for now. It's all a bit much for me, I realise, and I'm yearning for peace and quiet. But first I still have a little work to do. I walk to the local library and browse through the newspapers from the past week, then photocopy the items that carried information about the accident. Both environmentalists and politicians against the protection of the World Heritage listed Hinchinbrook Island have jumped on Warren's bandwagon, trying to steal the limelight to push their causes. I will put the copies in an envelope and add them to the sketches in Warren's bedside drawer. Somehow he will like to have this information when he's on the road to recovery back in Melbourne. He's probably being operated upon at this very moment . . .

A telephone call to the hospital explained that Warren was being 'opened up' again at 1.00pm. So I have nested myself in the grass of the Esplanade, close to the hospital and the landing strip of the QES rescue helicopter. Natalie has taken the train back to Brisbane.

Diary: The water on the edge of the mudflats is very calm. The wind plays with the leaves of a few short and stocky palm trees. At this side of the Esplanade there is little tourism. But hordes of joggers, skaters, the odd skateboarder and a few cyclists. I try to draw them but can't bring up the necessary concentration. So I write a few postcards. One to Jet, my girlfriend and one to my uncle Ad who has come through marrow transplantation which cured him from leukaemia. I feel a strong tie between us. The writing leads to another area in my mind and returns me to Hinchinbrook Island and especially the descent. I've been so occupied with Warren that I have neglected many of my own thoughts and slowly, as I lie in the sun, my mind remembers them and I note them here in my diary.

Parting once more

The visit to Warren in the afternoon was a long one. I arrived at 2.00pm and sat with him for an hour and a half. I asked permission from the nurse to sketch him and when he came out of his narcosis she relayed my question to him and he agreed. So I studied and drew his face. I was the only visitor. A thick furrow across his forehead explained that he was involved in yet another battle. He was very quiet and after he had come out of it his mood seemed much lower than I had previously witnessed. We didn't talk much. I was happy and content to be with him alone in this large quiet room. Slowly, however, my content mood made way for the reality of Warren's fate. I noticed that I started to look at him differently as the time passed, confronting myself now with an 'I'm sitting in his way' attitude. But Pat and Graeme Macdonald came to my rescue when they walked in shortly afterwards.

Warren's favourite drink was an apple, carrot and celery fruit juice, which his parents usually bought for him from a shop in town and this was a good opportunity for me to go and get one for him. This gave privacy to Warren and his parents and I could do something useful. But the shop had run out of apples and with no juice I returned to the hospital where it seemed he had overcome his depression and was fighting for his new life again.

At 5.30pm I had to say my goodbye to him and it was a difficult moment.

'I see you later, Warren.' I hugged him and I walked into the corridor where four family members were waiting to go in. I said goodbye to them as well and met Warren's parents outside on the lawn. I parted from them too. Emotionally touched, I walked to my hostel, where I cancelled the taxi that was going to take me to the bus terminal. I packed my stuff and walked instead, needing the physical exercise.

At the terminal I boarded a McCafferty bus and soon it drove out of Cairns, stopping, of course, in Cardwell where we took a 40 minute break. Once again I was confronted with a view of the island. A cool ocean breeze freshened my face. Let's hope that Warren's wounds and mine will heal. Maybe the salt that was rubbed into my wound by looking at the island would have a healing effect.

Reunited again

On May 2nd my flight back to Europe would depart from Cairns airport. Since the time I had said goodbye to Warren and now, there had been a few weeks in which I tried to get loose from the accident. I ate well and was spoiled by

Trish, who's a great cook, swam within the protection of the stinger nets off the Townsville beach and discussed my plans for the future.

Slowly my sleeping pattern started to come good and I think I was recuperating. An old friend of mine, Michael Matthews, lives and works on the aboriginal settlement on Palm Island. I decided to visit him and I had a few good days there, intending to stay a week but leaving much sooner as the music being played on the island was too loud for me. It seemed like every house had stereos with only one setting: 'Play It Loud'. I wanted to hide, I felt lost and I was on the run! From what?

But I had a few good days, thanks to the hospitality of Mike and the people he shared his house with, before returning to Rohan and Trish, in whose company I started to feel I was ready to go home.

Together we visited Magnetic Island, ate more exciting meals, talked heaps and I bought some souvenirs. I called the hospital in Cairns to see if there was a chance that Warren was still there. I had expected that he had been transferred to Melbourne but to my surprise and delight he was still in the Cairns Base Hospital.

Finally the day of my departure came and for the last time I took the bus to Cairns. Eating from a lunch packet made by Trish while it drove through the sugarcane fields of North Queensland, watching a video and once again stopping in Cardwell. After a good last look at the island I felt very relieved to leave it behind me.

At the hospital I found a sparkling Warren, with his happier and much more relaxed parents. He looked a lot better and talked a lot. Much of his wiring and tubing had disappeared and above his bed there was a construction from which he could pull himself up. It was fantastic to see him that way, full with new spirits. It would make my journey home a lot more pleasant, too. What a strong individual he was. Graeme took a photograph of us. A nice moment as Warren strongly held my hands. Then they left to give us some privacy. We talked about his experiences up on the mountain for a while. About the black ants in his groin, the noise of the water and the weather. The phantom pains he still felt and the yabby story.

Then I said goodbye for the last time — well, for the near future anyway — and walked out of the hospital where Pat and Graeme were waiting for me. Together we walked to the Esplanade and drank a cup of coffee. Then they dropped me off at my guesthouse and finally I said goodbye to these kind people too.

Malaysian Airlines soon took me away from Australia and brought me back to Europe. Three months had ended in a very disturbing fashion. When would I see Warren again? I know that I will be back one day.

FEVER, PAIN AND NIGHTMARES

My legs were far from the only casualty of the accident. Though most of the rock's weight had been taken by my legs, a significant amount rested in my lap. For a while at least, the pain in my legs took a back seat compared with what I was experiencing between them.

The pain was excruciating, like somebody had put a bowling ball in my crotch and, hanging onto both of my legs, was trying to force it up my arse with their foot. The pressure was incredible. My balls had swollen to the size of oranges and stretched my scrotum to the point where I thought it would split. However, it held firm, and in doing so, pushed my now enormous testes back into me. No amount of painkiller did anything to stem the pain. I seriously wanted the surgeons to cut them out and put them back in when the swelling went down! Surely they could do that. *This was the nineties, for Christ's sake!*

I felt like I needed to lie on my side in the foetal position to relieve the pain, but couldn't. My fractured pelvis prevented me from lying in any position except on my back. I lay there praying for sleep to take me away from the pain but it never came when I really needed it. Sweat rolled off me as I tensed from side to side, trying to relieve the pressure. A fever had me sweating so much throughout the night that my sheets had to be changed regularly, sometimes at 3.00 or 4.00am. I felt as though I was fighting a losing battle, and wondered if this whole thing could possibly get any worse.

From intensive care, I'd been moved temporarily into the coronary ward, until a bed became free in general. Lying on my stomach for the first time, I had fallen asleep and awoke in fright to the sounds of raised voices.

An old Italian man in the bed diagonally opposite me had a couple of visitors and they were in a heated argument. Their voices grew louder and more aggravated until I didn't want to look over there in case I was interfering. Sensing something was very wrong, I looked over to see one of them holding to the old man's throat what appeared to be a knife. I froze in fear.

What the hell's going on? This can't be happening?

I looked again, turning my head just slightly, and squeezed my eyes tightly shut at the confirmation. I wanted to call out, but couldn't. Never have I felt so utterly vulnerable, so helpless as I did at that moment. Lying on my stomach, I would not be able to defend myself in even the feeblest way. I couldn't even roll over without help! If I called out, surely they'd finish me as quickly as the old man. I lay there frozen, trembling inside as I tried to remain invisible, hoping they would take no notice and leave me alone.

The argument continued between the two men, the old man intervening at times, the knife still held to his throat, me almost holding my breath for fear of being noticed. At the sound of further commotion, I looked up in horror to see my brother Brett walk into the room. I tried to yell out to him but no sound came. I recoiled in horror as the man with the knife lunged towards him, grabbing him as he walked by, bringing the knife up to his throat.

'Brett! Nooooo!' I yelled out inside, no sound leaving my throat. 'Leave him alone!' I screamed, my voice left echoing off the other side of the door as my mind slammed closed, unable to deal with what I was seeing.

Suddenly I was wrenched back by someone's voice, one of the nurses. Startled, I turned quickly to the corner, eyes wide with sheer terror. There was nobody there except the old man, looking very much alive. I was delirious, racked with fear as I tried to describe what I'd seen.

'Where's my brother? Is he all right? Where is he? There was a knife!' I told her in hysterics.

She put her hand on my arm, trying to reassure me. 'It's OK. He hasn't been in here. No one has. You've been having a bad dream.'

'He was. I saw him. They had a knife!'

'It's OK. It's only a dream. He's all right,' she continued, but I wasn't having any of it.

'What if they come back! I've seen them, they'll come back for me!' I cried.

'No they won't. There hasn't been anyone here. You've been having a bad dream.'

'I can't stay here! You've got to get me out! Get me out of here!' I pleaded.

I stayed terrified. Hysterical, until finally, after five milligrams of Valium, I began to relax, drifting off into the relative sanctuary of sleep. Or did I? I don't know how much later it was when I woke again, but

I quickly recalled what had happened earlier, and couldn't believe I was still here, in the same room.

But I wasn't just in the same room. I was alone.

I am still here. No! I've got to get out. They're going to come back for me!

Looking around the dark, empty room, my gaze came to a sectioned off area behind a drawn curtain. *They could be hiding in there!* I tried not to look over, tried to put the whole thing out of my mind, but it was useless. I had only just decided to call out for the nurse when I sensed that someone was watching me. I tried not to look, but couldn't avert my eyes before they settled on the dark shadow in the folds of the curtain.

My heart skipped a beat at the sight of a dark face, clearly visible, peering at me from the shadows.

No! Leave me alone! What are you doing here? I didn't see anything.

I tried not to stare, terrified to let him know I'd seen him. I squeezed my eyes shut, praying that this couldn't be happening. *There's no one there. There can't be, can there?* Opening one eye ever so slightly, like you do when you're pretending you're asleep, I looked again. I could barely contain the sharp intake of breath, then held it there as the ball of fear in my stomach tightened. *He's there alright, staring straight back at me!* I was already terrified, but what happened next sent me over the edge. He blinked.

I couldn't move, couldn't even think any more. I'd ceased to exist, couldn't afford to exist while I lay open to whatever the intruder had in mind. Time stood still, the very air, the very fabric of existence frozen with me. It could have been minutes. It could have been hours, I will never know, before the sound of someone entering the room brought me back.

'How are we going over here now, feeling better?' the nurse asked casually, unaware of the danger.

'No, I'm not,' I managed to reply, my voice a thin whimper. 'I've got to tell you something.' I was too scared to cry out, to tell her out loud what was happening, for fear of provoking him. She wouldn't be able to stop him on her own, and when he'd finished with her, it would be my turn.

'What is it?' she asked, sensing the fear in my voice. 'What's the matter?'

'Please, come over here so I can tell you,' I pleaded with her, so scared now that the tears began to well in my eyes. She came up to the side of my bed and leant down. 'What is it, what's the matter?'

As quietly as I could, I whispered, 'You've got to get help. There's somebody in here who wants to kill me.'

Without flinching, she held my arm reassuringly, 'There's no one here going to hurt you, Warren. You've been having a bad dream.'

Glancing past her, back towards the curtains, I shuddered as the menacing face glared straight back at me. I gripped her arm and begged her, 'You've got to get help. You've got to get out of here. He'll kill you too!' Tears ran down my face.

'There's nobody here, Warren. I'll show you. Now, where did you say they were? Behind here?' She took hold of the curtain to draw it back.

'Yes,' I nodded. 'But don't do it! You need to get help!' I whispered loudly, trying not to be heard on the other side of that curtain.

With that she drew it back quickly. I had to turn away.

'See. There's nothing there,' she said, certain that this would convince me. But I was sure he would leap out at any moment, from deeper within the room while she had her back turned, for she was still facing me and hadn't really looked inside.

'No, he's in there,' I pleaded as she walked away, towards the door. 'Nooooo! Don't leave me here! You've got to get me out!'

As I cried after her, I looked back in terror to the partially exposed room behind the curtain, seeing all the dark spaces, the corners I couldn't see into, knowing he was still in there, waiting. I felt myself slipping away again, unable to deal with being left alone when I thought I'd been saved. Slipping, slipping into an icy void, surrounded by black.

Sleep offered me little sanctuary:

Lying in a half sleep, I could hear voices arguing in the corridor outside the ward. It sounded like my sister Michelle, telling someone off for reasons I couldn't make out. Their voices became louder and louder until they were screaming at each other. 'For Christ's sake, shut up! Stop arguing,' I screamed in my head, the voices getting louder.

It sounded like more people had become involved now, and the raised voices intensified into the sounds of a fight.

'Michelle, get out of here!' I screamed in my head. 'Get me out of here.' I lay frozen solid as what sounded like a full-scale riot erupted, first in the corridor outside, then throughout the whole hospital. I could hear windows being smashed, doors being kicked in, people running and screaming.

I lay completely still, too terrified to move. Completely helpless, totally at the mercy of anyone who should burst into the room. I began to retreat into myself, trying to pretend this wasn't happening.

I tried to imagine myself escaping somehow and, in an instant, I was pulling myself along on my stomach in a trench outside the hospital. I watched in horror as carloads of people pulled up outside the hospital, throwing rocks through the windows and fighting amongst themselves. *I hope Michelle got out of there*, was all I could think. *God, I hope no one else was in there!* I watched as the building caught fire and became an inferno. Sinking my face down into the dirt, shaking my head in denial, I prayed for some kind of release. For an end to the madness.

RETALIATION

The one thing that drove me on, more than anything else, was the need to regain control. For the first weeks, I could hardly move at all and had to be 'rolled' manually each time my sheets had to be changed. The indignity of having to be rolled over like that needs to be experienced to be understood. What made the prospect even more daunting for me was the incredible pain that my broken pelvis put me in every time I had to go through it. The nurses weren't allowed to do it themselves, and had to call in ward staff, or 'wardies', to do the rolling.

The majority of the staff taking care of me in Cairns treated me well. However, some of the wardies, a couple of them, treated me like a bag of meat — or, more accurately, a bag of shit. More intent on getting back for another game of table tennis, or maybe (heaven forbid) being five minutes late for 'smoko', they would roll me over like a side of beef, ignoring my pleas to take it easy. *I've got a broken pelvis for Christ's sake!*

I dreaded each time the nurse mentioned calling them to roll me, and began looking for a way to make them redundant. *I'm not having those bastards treat me like this forever.*

My bed had an overhead frame, the type used to attach pulleys to, for patients in traction. Looking up at the bar above my head, I had a plan. If I sat forward and reached up, I could just curl my fingers around it. *Right! That's it! You bastards are out of my life!*

I started reaching up and holding on to that bar whenever I could, for a little longer each time. Before long, I could raise myself slightly from the bed, but only for a few seconds. That was enough, though. The next time my sheets were due to be changed, and the nurse mentioned calling the wardies, I told her not to worry about it.

'I don't want them touching me again. We can do it this way,' and reached up for the bar, lifting myself off the sheets. I think she was impressed.

That single step forward gave me an incredible sense of satisfaction. I'd regained some control — a small amount, maybe, but it was a huge step towards getting back some of the freedom that I valued so much. The satisfaction of doing something for myself, not having to rely on someone else. That single decision in regaining control over one aspect of my life was to set the pattern for the rest of my recovery.

OK, let's do it. I want my life back!

THAT'S MY MATE!

I'd always been hard on myself, harder than anyone else could have been. I would get so disappointed in myself if I did something stupid or weak, usually punishing myself verbally at least.

While working in a pub in London, I'd gotten fairly pissed one night, having a few quiet ones after work. I just caught the last train at Waterloo station, thanking my lucky stars because I couldn't really afford to catch a cab home. I took a seat and settled back for the short ride to Clapham Junction, two stops away.

'C'mon, don't go to sleep. It's only two stops,' I told myself as my head slowly dropped towards my chest, only to jerk up suddenly when it got there. *Bloody hell! Five more minutes and you'll be there. Stay awake!*

My head snapped up, eyes wide as I realised I'd been asleep. *The station!* I jumped up and swung open the door, stepping out onto the platform as the train began moving again. *That was lucky*, I thought to myself, *I nearly missed it.* My thoughts of good fortune sank like the *Titanic* as my blurry eyes focused on the sign above me: 'Heathrow'!

'Jesus! How the hell did I get to Heathrow? I only closed my eyes for a minute!' I mumbled angrily to myself.

Walking along the platform, I came to a timetable. *Time? What time is it now?* Hanging overhead was a huge digital clock, its green display declaring '01:45'. I turned back to the timetable and scanned the rows and columns until they eventually told me what I already really knew. *That was the last train. Shit! You bloody idiot! What are you going to do now?*

I was so angry with myself, spitting and cursing as I walked along the platform and out into the street. What made me even angrier was the fact that this wasn't the first time it had happened. The last time I'd ended up out this way somewhere, it had cost me 30 pounds to catch a cab. *You're not doing that this time, mate! You're going to have to deal with it!*

I decided to find somewhere to sleep, and catch the first train home in the morning. Wandering around the shops, looking for a sheltered doorway to sleep in, I felt like a complete derelict. *You were stupid enough to do this again. You can put up with it!* I tried lying down on some cardboard boxes behind a pizza shop, but a cold wind had got there first, swirling all around me, making sleep impossible.

'Jesus Christ, it's cold!' I said out loud, starting to shiver now.

I made my way back to the station, hoping to find somewhere out of the bitter wind, but to no avail. Pacing up and down the platform, I spotted what looked like a shed further down the line, only just discernible in the mist that was quickly developing. I jumped off the end of the platform and made towards it, the fog deepening by the minute. It was a small wooden shed, probably for keeping tools in, or maybe housing some of the switch gear. I tried the handle, knowing full well it would be locked. I wasn't disappointed. I put my shoulder to it in frustration, and nearly fell inside as the door swung wide open. *Great security!* I thought as I stepped inside.

I quickly closed the door behind me, shutting out the icy breeze that swirled the mist in through the gap. In the dark I couldn't make out what was in there — and it didn't matter anyway; I had to get some sleep. I pulled the curtains off one window and spread them out on the floor. Then I took the curtains off the second window, lay down on my impromptu mattress and pulled the drapes over me like a blanket.

Curling up tight, my knees tucked right in up under my stomach, I was still cursing myself as I drifted into an uncomfortable slumber.

I woke the next morning, stiff with the cold, threw back the curtains (in an unconventional fashion), stood and stretched for a second before stepping outside. Thick fog filled the air, I couldn't even make out the platform I'd come from. I moved towards it anyway, following the tracks. I would have made quite a picture for those standing on the platform above me, waiting for their trains to work. Out of the fog I emerged, still in my work clothes (black pants, with white shirt and tie — under a heavy coat, luckily!). My eyes must have been barely open, my hair all over the place. I staggered to the end of the platform, climbed up onto it, then casually strolled in amongst the throng of commuters. *See*, I thought to myself. *It's OK. I'm one of you lot!*

Walking in the door at 7.25am, with just enough time to get changed for another day of tree planting, I found my flatmate, Simon, in the kitchen making tea.

'Hey! That's my mate! Good job son!' he greeted me enthusiastically in his rich Zimbabwean accent.

I stood like a zombie, not quite comprehending where he was coming from. Then the penny dropped. He was convinced I'd gotten lucky and had spent what turned out to be the coldest night that winter wrapped up in the arms of a new woman.

'Mate, believe me. Nothing could be further from the truth!'

REALISATION

Wheeling myself slowly into the bathroom, I caught my reflection in the mirror as I turned to close the door. *Jesus! My eyes! Look at my eyes!* The pupils had dilated with the morphine, giving me a manic, crazed look. I looked like a dead ringer for Charles Manson! No wonder I was freaking people out! Seeing myself in the chair like that, I realised for the first time how other people saw me now, how they would see me for the rest of my life. My head reeling at the realisation, I felt my heart sink as the consequences unfolded before me.

That's it, isn't it. This is a life sentence. This is how I'll look when I die. This is how my kids are going to see me. How will they cope, having an old man who's a freak? How will they feel when other kids at school laugh at me and point?

Removing the towel from my lap (it was too hot, and my body too swollen and sore, to wear anything else), I stared intently at the image before me, the image of me from the waist up. 'What do I really look like?' I wondered; then, with both hands on the armrests of the wheelchair, I raised myself up out of the seat. I stared in horror and disbelief.

Nothing could have prepared me for what I saw.

'Jesus Christ!' I gasped aloud.

The shock of seeing myself like that for the first time was overwhelming. The impact so strong. I'd been looking down my body at the place where my legs used to be for a few weeks now and had become accustomed to the sight. But this was something else. This was how other people saw me. I couldn't stop looking, fascinated that I could look like that, so utterly changed. My legs looked so much smaller now that I was seeing them in perspective with the rest of my body. All that remained were two stumps. They just hung there under me like two legs of lamb, as I held myself up. I could not take my eyes away. *It's no wonder people stare the way they do now.*

I had been using the wheelchair for a few days now but still hadn't comprehended the role it would play in the rest of my life. At first, I saw it only as a temporary tool to get me to the shower or the toilet. It felt awkward to use, and I was afraid of falling out of it. My fragility scared me. Every little bump I came across sent a jolt of pain through my legs. It wasn't long before I began to accept the inevitable: *This is it, mate. You are now, officially, a cripple.*

ENTER SUNSHINE

Finally, the day arrived when I got to leave the hospital building for the first time. With Dad pushing me, we made our way through the maze that was the hospital. Through corridors that all looked the same. Correct me if I'm wrong, not claiming to be an expert on hospitals, but aren't they all like this? A maze, to throw the dazed patient, already totally disorientated, into further confusion. Mum gave me a commentary along the way of the different wards I'd been in, where different things were, and so on. From the lift on the ground floor, Dad wheeled me out through the front glass doors and into the sunlight for the first time. My throat tightened as I came to grips with the fact that three weeks had passed since I had last seen the sun. It wasn't the emotion that had me squeezing my eyes tightly shut, though.

'That bloody sun's bright!' I complained as we crossed out from under the shade of the alcove. 'Jesus, I need some shades!'

My eyes had become used to the dim hospital lights and were knocked for six by the full glare of the midday sun in Cairns. We made a beeline for the shop in front of the hospital into which Mum darted and quickly returned with a bottle of mineral water (I was still constantly thirsty and hadn't thought to bring a drink bottle) and some sunglasses.

With the glare problem sorted out, I began to appreciate the heat of the sun as it beat down on me. It felt incredible on my skin after what seemed like a lifetime of lying in bed inside the dull confines of the hospital. Crossing the road to a stretch of parkland between the Esplanade and the sea, Dad pointed to a concrete pad set in the middle, with a path connecting it to the road.

'That's where the helicopter landed when they flew you here.' I didn't recognise it at all. I remembered feeling like we had landed on the roof of the hospital, not across the road from it.

We carried on along a path through the park, Dad pushing me the whole time. It felt so strange. I couldn't help thinking that it must have been nearly 30 years since he last pushed me like this — in a pram! I could not possibly conceive how he was feeling about pushing me along in a wheelchair now, but I soon lost that train of thought with what happened next:

Approaching another road to cross, I noticed the distinct lack of gentle slope in the path, the kerb dropping straight into the gutter. Wondering what we were going to do now, I almost shat myself at being suddenly tilted back, totally unexpectedly.

'Bloody hell!' I yelled out, holding on to the chair so tight that my knuckles must have been white. 'What are you doing?'

My cry must have scared Dad just as much as his quickly executed mono had me. 'Shit, sorry mate,' he apologised. 'Are you right?'

'Yeah, I suppose,' I answered, still shaking. 'I might have to change my jocks when we get back, but apart from that, I'm fine.' I felt extremely nervous at my newfound vulnerability, and found myself bracing anxiously at the next kerb. This time Dad gave me plenty of warning, and once we had dropped down onto the road, we all began to laugh.

Mum thought it was hilarious. Because she had been standing ahead, waiting for us, she could see both our faces. Dad's smiling face as he set about solving his first wheelchair problem, and the look of sheer terror on my face as I felt the chair tip out from under me! It must have been quite a sight! We were still laughing about it as we arrived back in the dreary scenario of E West ward, just in time for dinner.

PROGRESS AT LAST

Eventually my wounds had healed well enough for the dressings to be changed in the ward, whereas previously they'd only been done in theatre. Consequently, I hadn't actually seen my legs yet, only the shape of them wrapped in bandages. The nurse carefully unravelled the dressing of my right leg as I looked on with a combination of morbid fascination and something best described as revulsion.

What remained of my leg looked like something out of a horror movie. Rather than use a skin graft to close the wound, the normal procedure is to leave flaps of skin beyond the actual amputation site, and sew these together over the stump end. Because I'd had so many operations, there wasn't a lot of skin left to work with. Consequently, they'd had to stretch the two flaps together so tightly, that to keep the stitches from pulling through the skin, the fishing line (yep!) they'd used passed through a dozen pieces of what looked like plastic maca-roni. They acted as pressure dispersers, keeping the tension sutures from cutting through my flesh.

The visual effect could only be described as looking like something out of a Frankenstein movie. *Christ! I'm glad Mum's not here to see this!*

She did, though, a few days later, popping her head around the curtain as they changed my dressing, before I had a chance to warn her. I cringed as I watched her looking at my legs, almost feeling embarrassed by the revulsion I felt sure she'd feel. Much to my relief, she handled it much better than I thought she would.

'They're a bit of a mess, aren't they,' she remarked, biting her bottom lip in a look of concern and sympathy.

'They're not bad,' I insisted, breathing a sigh of relief that she had not been repulsed by the sight. Deep down, to me it signified an acceptance. The thought of having my own mother being repulsed by my new image would have devastated me. Thankfully, it was a thought I could put out of my mind.

By the time the third week came around, I could finally see some light at the end of the tunnel. Arrangements were being made to get me admitted to a hospital back down in Melbourne, and I hadn't had any surgery for over a week! My appetite had returned, although I think that had something to do with the nutritionist recommending that, if I did not start eating more protein, they would have to recommence nightly drip feeds via a nasal tube. *No thanks! I think I feel hungry again now!*

My strength was improving also. I could do a couple of chin-ups on the bar above my bed, and, shuffling across the bed on my bum, get in and out of the wheelchair. When it was suggested that I spend some time sitting in the chair to prepare me for the flight to Melbourne, I thought it was a bit of a joke. *Practise sitting down! Yeah right, what do they think I am!*

I had never actually thought about gravity much before that day. Apart from its habit of holding you to the ground, or sending you crashing into it when its effect is deviously doubled with alcohol consumption, it had usually remained inconspicuous. Until I'd been flat on my back for three weeks, that is! After a mere ten minutes' sitting in the chair, I couldn't believe how tired I would become. I could feel the weight of every organ hanging in my chest, as if I was being pulled to the ground by my insides. I sat slumped in the chair for another five minutes before having to climb wearily into bed. I felt like a 90 year-old man, for Christ's sake. 'How long does it take to fly to Melbourne?' I asked Dad during an afternoon's 'sit'.

He replied, 'About four hours.'

'Great! Looks like I've got some training to do.'

HOME

Friday, May 9th 1997. Mum's birthday. What better present could she have hoped for? The day had finally arrived. I had been declared 'fit to fly', and the three of us would be flying home at 9.00pm.

For the most part, the day dragged on like any other, until the mad rush began at about 6.00pm. The nurse, doing my final change of dressings, stuffed around as if she had all day. Leaving them until way too late, we were left with little time to spare as we raced to the taxi stand in front of the hospital to find . . . no taxi. Dad was ropeable. He stormed off to find a telephone, and had the driver back there a few minutes later.

We finally arrived at the airport after having to endure the driver's whingeing about how he always has to wait for people. *Yeah, yeah.* I thought to myself, *I would like to have a dollar for every hour I've spent waiting for taxis in my life. I'd be flying home in a Lear jet!*

Paul and Karen were waiting out the front of the airport terminal when we arrived. They'd been fantastic, looking after Mum and Dad the whole time, giving them much needed space and support. I thanked them both as I transferred into another wheelchair, an extremely narrow one without armrests, designed for moving down aircraft aisles. A Qantas steward began wheeling me towards the gate. I felt uneasy without the armrests, worried I would lose my balance and fall out. The last thing I needed right now would be to damage my legs. I'd spent all the time I wanted, and more, in the Cairns Base Hospital.

There couldn't have been more than 50 people on board the plane, including the pilots and cabin crew. The flight had begun in Osaka and this was its only stop before arriving in Melbourne.

Down the aisle I'm wheeled, towards the back of the plane. Halfway down, we reach my seat, all nine of them. The seat backs are folded forward, so that the stretcher can rest on top, at about elbow height. This puts me up under the console, directly under the lights and switches. Facing the back of the plane, all I can see are empty seats. All the other passengers are seated up towards the front of the plane, behind me.

Nervous thoughts filled my head of what would happen if something went wrong, and we had to evacuate the plane. I had visions of people screaming and rushing for the exit doors as the plane burst into flames, leaving me strapped in, unable to escape. I felt incredibly vulnerable yet again, something I suspected I was going to have to get used to.

Surely nothing could happen to me now. I reassured myself. Not after everything I'd been through. *Could any god, or dealer of fate, be so cruel as to have me die in a plane crash now? After all that I've been through?* I hoped not. Sensing my anxiety, one of the flight stewards took the time to assure me that they would indeed get me out if an emergency arose.

As the front wheel lifted off the ground, I closed my eyes and succumbed to a relative calm. *I was going home.* What lay ahead of me, I didn't know, but that had never worried me in the past, and it didn't concern me now. I was alive after coming so close to death that I smelt like it. And I was heading home. Now I was starting to get somewhere.

PART 3 THE RECLAMATION

'In wilderness is the preservation of Mankind.'

Henry Thoreau

TALBOT

I was admitted to the Royal Talbot Rehabilitation Centre at about 2.00am Saturday morning, having come straight from Melbourne Airport. The whole family had been there to greet us. Lisa and Michelle had organised a wheelchair for me, and a disabled taxi stood waiting as we left the terminal. We travelled in convoy, Mum and I in the taxi, the rest of the family in two cars behind us.

I really didn't have any idea what lay in store for me at the rehab centre. Sitting in the taxi, staring blankly out the window, all I wanted was some idea of what I could do. Some kind of direction. Until now it had all been about recovery. I wanted to do *more* than recover. I wanted to know what my limits were. *Had I been reduced to sitting up in one of these things every time I needed to go somewhere?* So far, I had found no answers.

We'd been assured that somebody would be there to admit me, but the place looked deserted when we arrived. Mum finally found an intercom, and within a few minutes, a small Asian woman appeared. She opened the huge glass door, ushering us all inside. As you would expect at that hour of the morning, the place was deathly silent. I followed her down a corridor, everybody else behind me, until she stopped in front of a doorway to the left, motioning me inside.

'Your bed is in here,' she said quietly.

'No worries. Whereabouts?' I asked, poised in the doorway, my eyes still adjusting to the darkness.

'This way,' she replied, and I followed her to a bed in the far corner of the room, past half a dozen others that appear occupied. 'Here,' she said.

I thanked her, then turned back towards the door.

'Do you need some help to get in?' she asked, throwing me completely. My family were still waiting at the door. As if I was going to just wheel over and hop into bed, without even saying goodbye!

'No, I don't,' I replied. 'I need a coffee or something first. I haven't even said goodbye to these guys yet.'

'Ah, yes. OK,' she replied, and directed us into the communal dining/lounge area. After a quick coffee (the silence of a hospital at 2.30am isn't the most relaxing atmosphere in which to sit and chat), we said our goodbyes, and I made my way back to bed.

So began what would be a seven-month stay in the Royal Talbot.

The thing that struck me first upon waking in the morning was the feeling that I'd moved into a nursing home. Of the five guys in my room, two of them looked like they wouldn't live to see the sun go down.

Being a Saturday, nothing was happening as patients sat around, left to their own resources. I learnt that, come Monday, I would meet with the team assigned to rehabilitate me. In the meantime, an interim doctor paid me a visit, going through my medical history before asking me the million-dollar question:

'So, what do you hope to achieve in here Warren? What is your goal?'

I knew what I wanted to do. I'd known that right from the start, but I hadn't really talked about it with anyone until now.

'I want to walk again,' I answered, matter-of-factly.

'Mmmmm,' he replied, hand under his chin. 'That's going to be very difficult you know, Warren. It will take a lot of work.'

'Yeah, I reckon it will.' I was taken aback by his response.

'You see, it takes an incredible amount of effort to walk as an above knee amputee. I've seen the results of a study that concluded an above knee amputee uses up to two hundred per cent more energy than an average person just to walk,' he reasoned, obviously warning me not to get my hopes up too high.

'Mate, I'll be happy enough just to walk out of here,' I came back. 'What happens after that, we'll have to wait and see.' I didn't like his attitude in trying to quash my aspirations, and his suggestion to me that I might not be able to walk triggered a desire to prove him wrong.

He continued, 'See, your stumps are very short. You may not be able to use prostheses at all. We'll have to wait and see what the prosthetist says, whether he thinks he'll be able to help you.'

Nobody had raised the issue of the length of my stumps until now; I had just presumed it would be a matter of a lot of hard work before I walked again. After he'd left, I lay back on my bed, head swimming at the notion that I may not be able to walk again. The thought dragged me down like a lead weight tied around my neck, placing a black cloud that would hang over me until my appointment with the prosthetist, scheduled for Monday morning. Until then I explored around the hospital, getting used to moving about in the wheelchair.

It wasn't long before I met another couple of young blokes, helping me feel a bit more at home, not so out of place. Dallas was a great bloke who had been doing it pretty hard over the last few years. His body had basically given up on him after years of neglect, and refused to go any more. Mark had ridden his motorbike into the front of a truck, smashing one leg up so badly he almost lost it. The three of us, later joined by Lloyd, would be spending a fair bit of time together over the coming months, sneaking out for a pizza and a few beers every now and then.

Monday morning. The five members of my rehabilitation team all gathered around my bed: Jeanett Hofland, the doctor in charge of the amputee unit. John Semmens, the prosthetist. Liz Howard, my occupational therapist. Belinda Walsh, my physiotherapist, and the amputee units nurse, whose name I can't remember.

The curtain was drawn around me before the nurse began removing my dressings. I felt extremely nervous — not because of the attention to my wounds (I was used to that by now); it was the consequences of what it would mean if John decided he couldn't help me that worried me. The relief that swept over me when he leant forward, took a good look at my stumps and proclaimed 'Yeah, I reckon we can do something with that' was enormous.

OK then. That's all I need to hear!

I threw myself into rehab like a man possessed. I had to give myself the best possible chance of success, and that would mean being as fit as I could possibly be. Wheeling into the amputee gym, I was startled at first by the sight of all these people with various missing limbs. Then again, I probably freaked them all out as well; they *all* had more in the leg department than I'd been left with.

The first objective was to get my balance back. As you may be able to imagine, losing so much weight in the form of my legs threw my balance out completely. I had to be very careful just sitting up, that I didn't topple over backwards!

We started with me sitting up on a treatment bed and Belinda standing in front of me, throwing a tennis ball between us. When that got too easy, we moved on to using bats, turning the exercise into a form of aerial table tennis. From there, we moved on to a medicine ball. Now that was interesting! The first time she threw it to me, it knocked me over backwards! However, the workout it gave my stomach muscles was incredible. When I caught it off to one side, I spun around with it, carried through by the ball's momentum. I thought I was doing well with all this balance stuff, until she brought over the 'fit' ball and told me what she wanted me to do!

Easing myself off the edge of the bed, Belinda on one side of me and Allison (my second physiotherapist), on the other, I sat on top of this high pressure ball and my stomach tensed as it moved about. Suddenly, it rolled from under me. Too slow to throw my hips forward, I had to be grabbed by the girls to keep me from falling. It gave me quite a start, my stomach still doing cartwheels as they helped me back on.

'Yeah right! Great game, this is!' I laughed, sure that they'd set me an impossible task.

'You'll be alright.' Belinda assured me, having a bit of a giggle herself. 'That was good. I think you'll do really well on this.'

At the same time, I began using what is commonly known as a 'wobble board'. Consisting of a 20 millimetre plywood disc about 400 millimetres in diameter, which is screwed on to a wooden hemisphere about 150 millimetres in diameter, the wobble board became my favourite toy. Placed on the floor, hemisphere side down, it presented an extremely unstable seat. Just being able to sit on it was an achievement in itself. In the beginning, I couldn't stay on it for more than a few seconds before falling off. It, too, gave my stomach muscles an incredible workout. That alone was incentive enough for me to get on it at every opportunity. I had become resigned to the fact that, because I spent so much time sitting down, the spare tyre around my waist was now part of the furniture. The wobble board provided a glimmer of hope that maybe, just maybe ...

The only thing holding me back now was a wound at the back of my left stump that still hadn't healed. It had begun as a graze, possibly from the initial impact of hitting the river bed under the rock. In Cairns it turned into a bed sore and became infected. Until it had healed to a point that the doctors were happy with, I would not be able to begin prosthetic training. I vented my frustration through exercise, becoming obsessed with getting stronger. In the amputee gym, I had a program of exercises designed to get me strong enough to handle the force that my body would have to endure.

My back, especially, concerned me. If there was one thing that could stop me from walking again, that was it. I had incorporated some basic yoga into my routine also. It must have been quite a sight for visitors to the gym to be greeted by the sight of a legless man in a shoulder stand at the back of the room! Each afternoon I went through another set program of weight work in the main gym, run by Wayne Dite. I think Wayne got a kick out of having someone using the gym the way I did. My attitude was markedly different from that of his average customers; a lot of them were there under duress, having to be pushed along reluctantly for their own benefit. I was on a mission! I wanted to get myself into the best possible shape so that when the time came to walk again, my body would be ready. Only forces outside my control would be able to stop me. I had always had to work extremely hard to stay fit. Now, without being able to walk, I found it even harder; no matter how much exercise I did, I always felt like I needed more.

'I really need to be swimming,' I kept saying to anyone who would listen, convinced it was my aerobic fitness that was letting me down. But I wouldn't be able to start swimming until my wound had healed; it was deemed too risky for me to swim in the hydrotherapy pool with an open wound, for my health and that of others.

There was talk that, when I was ready to use the pool, I would have to be lowered into the water on a hoist, for safety reasons. Nobody could tell me what my buoyancy would be like, but it didn't matter to me.

'Sorry, but you can forget that,' I replied. I wasn't about to suffer the indignity of being lowered into the pool like a rescued whale — not after having read how Douglas Bader went about his first swim after losing both legs in an aircraft accident: after pulling himself up the ladder rungs of the diving tower, he dragged himself to the end of the board, went into a handstand, then dived off.

'No, I'll be going in off the side, at the very least. That, or I'll go and swim somewhere else.'

LOOKING FORWARD

After the first couple of weeks, it was decided I was well enough to go home on the weekends. The doctors had agreed that Michelle could change my wound dressings — which, thankfully, she had volunteered to do — so that I could spend the weekends at home with Mum and Dad. Dad fixed a couple of handrails in the toilet, and we had to borrow some ramps for me to get up to the back door until my sister's partner, Per, made up a set at work.

It felt so good coming up the driveway to our house, like another piece of my life had fallen back into place. Sitting at the kitchen table with Mum and Dad was such a simple act, yet symbolised my return in a grand way. I was starting to feel like a normal person again. Being in hospital tends to strip away your character. You start to mould to the form of a 'patient'. I think it's got something to do with being surrounded by sick people; unless you really fight it, the sombre atmosphere can drag you down with it.

I decided early on that I needed to be able to get in and out of my chair from the floor. I practised in the amputee gym, starting with steps first. Sitting with my back to a single step, both hands on top of it behind me, I lifted my bum up using my triceps, dragging it up and over onto the step. Gradually, we increased the height, but this still seemed like a difficult way to go about it. One night, sitting on the lounge room floor at Mum and Dad's, an idea came to me. Sitting in front of the wheelchair, side on, I kept my left hand on the front of the chair, but put my right hand on the floor. Leaning forward, moving my weight over my right hand, I lifted my bum into the air, steadying myself with my left hand. I held myself there for a second before swinging my body up and across, catching the edge of the seat under my bum.

Yes! That's it! I've got it!

The feeling was electric. I sensed the implications immediately. I was no longer 'confined' to the wheelchair. I could get out and get back in again when I pleased. I could leave it behind if it got in the way. It was my first taste of freedom in a long time, a huge step forward.

When somebody suggested that I might see the hospital's psychologist, I was a little put out at first.

'What, do you think I'm going to lose the plot or something?' was my initial response.

'No. It's a standard requirement in everyone's rehabilitation. Just to make sure you're coping with things mentally as well as physically,' came the retort.

'OK, then.' *This should be interesting.*

Expecting some middle-aged, tweed jacketed, pipe smoking eccentric, I was pleasantly surprised to meet Daphne Smith, my psychologist. On our first meeting, although we just chatted casually, telling stories about what we had done and where we'd been, I felt very much on guard. I figured a psychologist's job was to take you apart piece by piece and then put you back together again. A bit dramatic I know, but that's how I felt!

At my next appointment, I began to relax, and eventually started to look forward to our meetings. They gave me a chance to talk to somebody, not in the 'purging my soul' sense, but in talking to someone who seemed interested in what I had done, how I was coping now, what I wanted to do, and so on...

Eventually her contract ran out — money was short and apparently the patients' mental health wasn't really that important. I kept in touch with Daphne outside of the hospital, gaining strength from her encouragement and support.

BACK ATTACK

The time I spent campaigning in the Tarkine taught me what I really wanted to do with my life. I decided that the only way we could get people to value wilderness was to show it to them. Not on TV, but by taking them into it. Giving them a taste of what I felt every time I walked out into the bush, the rejuvenation I felt at being immersed in nature.

Once the Donaldson River Bridge had been built, and we realised that stage of the battle had been lost, I became thoroughly disillusioned with everything. What had we achieved? Anything? It took me a while to appreciate we had. There wasn't a single person left in Tasmania now who hadn't heard of the Tarkine, and that wouldn't have happened if we had stood quietly by. What we needed to do now was *show* it to them. And who was in a better position to do that than us, the Tarkine

Tigers, who had fought so hard to save it? We even had our own tracks that nobody else knew about. But first, it was time to rest. Time to recoup some energy after our enormous struggle.

I spent a couple of weeks travelling around the state, sleeping under the stars at Sisters Beach on the north coast, exploring new forests, swimming in wild rivers. Jarrah, whom I'd first met on the Roger trip, had told me one night about a course he was thinking of doing. An 'adventure tour guides' course that would give him the qualifications to work in the industry. It sounded like an excellent idea. If we were going to set up ourselves, running trips through the Tarkine, it made sense to have some recognised qualifications. I doubt that any government agency would approve of experience gained in activities carried out in opposition to their policy. After all, we had cost them a hell of a lot of money!

Meanwhile, I'd gone completely into relaxed mode, and had forgotten all about the course. One evening, sitting around the table in a hut high on Mount Dundas, in the state's west, Jarrah casually mentioned that applications for the course closed the next day, at midday.

'Tomorrow?' I asked.

'Yeah, I think it's tomorrow,' he replied.

'Shit. We'd better get down there then.'

First thing in the morning, three of us packed and hiked back down the mountain. Jarrah, myself and Andrew Devine. Andrew was keen to do the course also, with plenty of enthusiasm and experience for his young age. We drove into the nearest town, Zeehan (an old mining town), had no trouble finding the post office (it's a small town!), and used the phone to ring the number Jarrah had been given. A guy called Brian Hall was running the course. He said we needed to complete an application form, which was no problem — he could fax one to us. *Excellent!*

As soon as the fax came through, we found a place to have breakfast, filling in our applications over toast and coffee. We then faxed the forms back to Brian and rang him to make sure he had received them.

That afternoon we drove to Devonport for an interview the following day. I hit it off well with Brian straight away. Built like a brick shithouse, he had that unique mix of professionalism and fun, always smiling. I felt I stood a good chance of getting in to the course; and sure enough, Jarrah and I started it a week later, with Andrew missing out because of his age. It became clear to me almost immediately that this was what I wanted to do — this was what I'd been heading towards for some time now, and I had finally arrived.

We devoted the next month to learning the commercial side of adventure travel. Then we spent a couple of days rafting on the Upper Mersey River, and some time around Cradle Mountain, climbing to its summit one glorious afternoon. After that, we had a break of four weeks before the next session began, so I figured this to be a good opportunity to catch up with family and friends back in Melbourne and Brisbane. I had been away for a year.

When I rang Brian from Melbourne one afternoon to confirm the starting date, he told me the bad news. We'd just had a federal election and with the change in government, all funding for Skillshare courses had been temporarily frozen. That included ours.

'Give me a ring in another few weeks, Waz. Something may have happened by then,' he advised, disappointment in his voice.

So I did, but by then the news was even worse. The course funding had been frozen indefinitely. It looked likely to be scrapped altogether. After my initial disappointment, I decided that I would go back to Tassie and do the courses I needed to do privately. It was going to cost me a fair bit of money, which I didn't have, and with winter coming on I couldn't expect to rely on painting work down in Tassie. I rang Athos Venturi, a landscaping contractor I'd worked for a few years before in Melbourne.

'Yeah, mate. I reckon I might have some work for you,' he said.

'Excellent! When can I start?'

I worked for Athos for the next few months, at one stage using a Bobcat (a small, skid-steer earthmover) to shift topsoil on a building site. I must have had a stupid grin on my face whenever I drove that Bobcat. Only months before, in the Tarkine, I'd been arrested after having to be cut from beneath a bulldozer with an angle grinder. I found it quite bizarre now to be using the tools of the 'enemy'.

The money was beginning to build up; it wouldn't be long before I could head back down to Tassie and get on with it. My back had been getting sore and stiff in the winter cold. I figured it just meant I was getting too old for this caper, too weak. Then, one morning I had trouble reaching down to pull my boots on, pain stabbing into my back. Ambling into work, I said to Ath's partner, Tony:

'Mate, I hope you haven't got much planned for today, because I'm not gonna be worth two bob.' I told him what the problem was, and made sure he gave me all the easy jobs to do for the day. But it wasn't enough. I woke the next day in agony, finding it difficult to get out of bed. Now I couldn't reach my feet at all.

I felt like something was badly wrong, the pain unlike anything I'd felt before. It felt like something inside was physically restricting my movement. I made an appointment with a local GP who sent me off to have some X-rays done. Back at the doctor's for the results, I sat and listened as he brought my world undone with his news. He explained that I had done some damage to one of the discs in my back. He didn't think my injury was that bad — as long as I didn't lift anything heavy, I would be fine. I sat there astounded.

'Not that bad? Were you listening when I told you what I do for a living. What I plan to do for a living?' I responded angrily.

'People have much worse injuries,' he replied.

'I'm sure they do. But they're probably sitting at home right now on the couch, watching TV!'

I left the clinic absolutely shattered, my head swimming at the very thought of things I wouldn't be able to do. *I'll never be able to carry a backpack again,* I thought, the concept tearing my heart out. *How am I going to travel if I can't pick up any kind of work?* My whole lifestyle revolved around freedom, being able to come and go as I pleased, picking up work whenever I needed it. I couldn't imagine what I'd do with that freedom taken from me. *That's it mate. You're finished!*

Over the following weeks I sank into a downward spiral of depression at the uncertainty that lay ahead. I had never had to face anything like this before. Sure, I'd been injured — but always temporarily. I'd never had to face the prospect of not being able to do something ever again, and facing that reality now terrified me.

At Mum's suggestion, I saw a physiotherapist. He made the situation very clear for me, giving me some badly needed hope. He mentioned a footballer who carried much the same injury as mine.

'He never gets to play the whole season, and he puts in a hell of a lot of work to play the games he does. But he plays.'

That was all I needed to hear. *If anyone with a damaged disc can run around a football field like those mad bastards do, I can carry a pack!* He gave me a series of stretches and exercises to do, and suggested I swim as often as possible. I immediately swung into action, desperate to get my life back. After a month, I figured 'Why go through this recuperation in a depressing Melbourne winter when I can be back up north in the sunshine?'

I planned to get myself back into shape, enjoying the sunshine at the same time, then head back down to Tassie when I was ready. Destiny, however, had other plans...

I'm sure now that going through that experience with my back helped me cope with losing my legs. I know it might be hard to understand how, but think of it this way. When I first injured my back, I thought my life as I knew it was over. And in a way, it was. Although not as restricted as I had initially thought, that injury did limit what I would be able to do. Forever. Therefore, I had already gone through some of that pain, that mental anguish of having had something taken away from me — albeit as a fraction of what was to come, but I went through it nevertheless.

DRIVING

The next step in my regaining my freedom was to start driving again. My occupational therapist made arrangements for a driving lesson with a company that has cars fitted out with hand controls.

Sliding out of my chair and in behind the wheel felt so bizarre. I put my seat belt on, and as I did the buckle up, I looked down at the gap from the pedals on the floor to my thighs. It was one of those moments when everything came back to me: the stark reality of, *yes, you've got no legs*. I tried to picture my legs reaching down to the pedals but couldn't. I know it sounds insane, but the distance seemed too great, I could not imagine my legs ever having been long enough to reach the pedals. Hell, I wasn't even sure where my knees had been!

Pulling out into the stream of traffic, I was amazed at how confident I felt. It really wasn't as difficult as I had first imagined. I'd had visions of the absolutely hopeless scenario of trying to go for the brake pedal with the foot that isn't there.

I drove with the instructor for 45 minutes around the streets of Northcote and Preston before returning to the Talbot.

'Well, how did I go?' I asked.

'No problems at all,' he replied, and that was it.

My car was on the back of a truck, being shipped down from Northern Queensland. Rob Baines, the painting contractor I'd been working for at the time of the accident, had brought it back from Cardwell. I'd left it parked behind the ferry office to pick up on my return from the island.

As soon as my car arrived in Melbourne, I arranged for it to be converted. Driving it again for the first time was incredible. Driving over to visit Lisa and Per one Friday night, I almost felt normal again. As I sat at the traffic lights, I thought of how I must look to other drivers. How normal I must look. I felt in a way that I was deceiving them, going under false pretences. I dreaded more than anything the prospect of having an accident, that I may be looked upon as someone who 'shouldn't have been driving anyway'.

In a mischievous way, I looked forward to picking up my first hitchhiker!

THE FIRST STEP

On June 24th, just ten weeks after losing my legs, I stood up again for the first time. John stood before me, within the parallel bars, while Allison stood behind. Everyone in the room had stopped what they were doing and was watching, waiting. With one hand on each of the bars, leaning forwards, sitting on the edge of my wheelchair seat, I heaved myself up between them. Straightening my stumps as they rode up in their new sockets, I felt the titanium knees snap into place underneath me.

'How does that feel?' John asked, eyes level with mine for the first time.

Relaxing my arms slightly, I let my legs take a little more weight, completely absorbed by the incredible feeling of standing again. It was some moments before I managed to answer.

'Pretty good,' I replied, always the champion of the understatement, an uncontrollable grin the only indication of the excitement that boiled up within me.

I felt an overwhelming sense of pride that they were seeing the real me at last. That, for that moment, they saw past the image of the cripple, and caught a glimpse of me as the real person. The way I had been. The way I still felt inside. I felt like I was showing them my most prized possession, and their smiles of appreciation had me battling to control my emotion.

As I stood savouring all these incredible feelings, John got to work with his allen key, readjusting the alignment of my knees and ankles. Around my waist, I wore a plastic brace, complete with six-pack abs. Fixed to my laminate sockets with hinged metal braces, it acted like a splint, supporting my torso in case my hips were incapable of doing so.

Standing back in front of me again, John said, 'There you go, try that. Let's see if you can take a few steps.' I looked up in surprise, my excitement tainted with uncertainty.

'Can I?' I asked, still getting used to the idea that I was actually standing. I hadn't dared let my mind wander any further forward — the enormity of the moment wouldn't allow it.

'I don't see why not,' he answered. 'We're both here to catch you.' Allison moved my wheelchair so she could get in behind me.

'I've got your knees adjusted for maximum safety so you will probably have trouble breaking them,' John began, explaining how the knee is meant to be snapped open upon stepping forward. Then, after swinging it through underneath, you snap it closed with the help of a return spring, allowing it to be safely stepped onto. 'For now, just try and walk with straight legs.'

'Cowboy style?' I suggested, smiling at the thought.

'Yeah, something like that,' he laughed.

Taking more weight through my arms again, I lifted my right hip, tilting my pelvis until one paint-spattered sandshoe left the floor. (These work shoes got a few laughs, but were comfortable.) I swung the heavy prosthesis forward with the little leverage my stump provided and, twisting my hips, stepped onto it. Juggling my weight between it and my arms, I swung my left leg forward, bringing it down just in front of the right. Lifting myself with the bars, I stepped back slightly to get my balance. As I drew in a deep breath, Neil Armstrong's famous words from 1969 echoed through my mind. 'One small step for a man...'

I had taken my first step.

ANOTHER OPERATION

I had become increasingly disillusioned with the progress of my left stump. Although the wound underneath didn't stop me from walking, it seemed not to be healing at all. In fact, I tried to avoid believing it, but it actually seemed to be getting worse. It was healing from the sides in, rather than from the bottom up. Although the surface hole was barely big enough to fit a matchstick into, it was still about 1.5 centimetres deep. I feared that it could be getting deeper. I was worried about the fact that it was taking so long to heal, but was constantly reassured that it would be OK.

The prospect of another operation, losing more of my leg, chilled me. I could not think about it without sinking into a pit of depression. *Will this ever be over?* I tried to convince myself there wasn't a problem; that the doctors knew what they were doing, and worrying about it would only make things worse. Working on the theory that, if you dwell on the negative aspects of something for too long, you could actually be making it worse. Manifesting something that wasn't there to begin with. In hindsight, I wish I had followed my gut feeling, but *hindsight* is just that.

When it finally became obvious that it wasn't going to heal, arrangements were made for me to have a Sinu-gram — a test in which the wound cavity is filled with Contrast, a liquid that shows up in an X-ray. This is done to determine whether the wound may be 'tracking' (the infection spreading deeper into the tissue, complicated by the wound healing at the surface).

As I lay on the X-ray bench, watching the image of my leg on the monitor while the Contrast was being injected, my heart sank at the sight of a white stain spreading slowly as it filled the cavity.

'Jesus!' I spat out aloud. 'I knew it!' I was so angry — with myself mainly, for not acting on my gut instinct; but also at the way in which this had been allowed to get so far, that the health system operates on a wait-and-see basis rather than a preventive one. The main fissure had got to within a few millimetres of my femur. If it had made the distance, the infection would have entered the bone, and I would have lost the majority of what remained of my left leg. At that moment, I lost any faith I had in the medical profession whatsoever.

Ten days later, on Friday July 25th, I went into the Austin Hospital for day surgery. I left that afternoon with a hole underneath my left leg that was 5 by 10 centimetres in area and 7.5 centimetres deep.

Dad and Michelle picked me up, driving me home for the weekend. Michelle had been changing my dressings on the weekends, so she had come along to be briefed on my post-operation dressing requirements. This allowed me to go home, rather than spend the weekend in the Royal Talbot. Feeling no pain as I left, I tossed the packet of Panadol the nurse had given me onto the dashboard of the car. As the anaesthetic began to wear off that evening, a dull, throbbing ache developed that became so intense that I had trouble sleeping. By morning it had reached the point where it could not be contained by strong pain killers and I began to wonder why my dosage of morphine hadn't been raised (I was almost weaned off it by then).

Michelle came around to Mum and Dad's the following day to change the dressing. Unwrapping the bandages, she gasped aloud at the size of the wound. While I was under the anaesthetic it had been packed so tightly with saline soaked gauze that *she* now had trouble getting it out. *I* had trouble staying conscious.

Even after everything I had been through, the pain I felt as Michelle pulled those dressings out was unbearable. It felt like she was pulling the very bone out of my leg. Head thrown back, I rocked in agony as she removed each piece, each one deeper and tighter than the last. Grimacing, she shared my pain as she pulled, distraught at having to cause me so much agony. We both knew all too well that the packing had to come out, and I knew by the expression on her face that what lay underneath didn't look good. She had seen some serious stuff in her time, but she could not believe the size of the hole they had left in me. Neither could I, when I used a mirror to look at it. So deep that

I needed a torch to see right into it, the hole was big enough to accommodate a small fist. My stomach churned at the sight, my head spinning with the thought of how long it would take to heal.

For eight weeks the wound required dressing every day, sometimes twice. It would be three months before I could walk again, or swim, so I spent all of my time in the gym. I was determined not to let this set-back slow me down any more than necessary, and took the opportunity to spend a week in Tassie while recuperating. The trip empowered me tremendously, reinforcing my independence as I drove around the state alone. I was back on the road. Back in control of my destiny.

THE COPTER RETURNS

While waiting for my wound to heal, it seemed like a good idea to learn how to use my wheelchair properly. After each afternoon's work-out in the gym, Wayne began teaching me the skills I would need to survive in the wheelchair unfriendly world outside the Talbot's walls.

First, he taught me how to do a 'mono' (balancing on the rear wheels only — either moving or still), spending what seemed like hours standing behind to catch me each time I overbalanced. From there, I learnt how to get up and down kerbs and gutters, practising first on wooden platforms inside the gym. I kept Wayne amused with my weekly tales of spills taken over the weekend. Like the time I'd taken a swan dive onto the doorstep of the local video shop. My brother Brett was taken completely by surprise as I went about show-ing him how I could get up steps now. I pushed down so hard on the push-rims that my bum came up out of the seat beneath me, sending me sliding down the front of the chair, chest first onto the doorstep!

My mobility increasing, I started spending more time away from the hospital. During the week, I would often meet friends for dinner, usually at my newfound second home, 'The Vegie Bar' in Fitzroy's Brunswick Street. Leaving the restaurant after dinner with Daphne one night, I stopped as I heard a sound in the distance. I just sat there as the memories flooded back, the whirring hum of the helicopter's rotors moving closer. I thought of how much I'd wanted to hear that sound the whole time I had spent trapped. The feeling of disbelief when the sound eventually came, holding my breath, not daring to believe they were heading my way. How I'd felt when I finally saw it, a black, buzzing spot in the distance, flying towards me. Tears threatened to squeeze from my eyes as I scanned the night sky, anxious to see it.

'Are you OK?' Daphne asked.

'Yeah,' I replied with a lump in my throat. 'That's the first time I've seen a helicopter since Hinchinbrook.' I was still gazing skyward, not wanting her to see the tears welling in my eyes.

'How does it feel?' she asked.

'Like I'll always remember that sound as the turning point in my life,' I said quietly, my voice trembling. 'Until I heard that helicopter, I'd all but given up. I'd prepared myself to die. Hearing that helicopter, meant that I still had a chance when I'd given up all hope.'

A single tear traced its way down my face as the drone of the rotors moved off into the night.

OFF THE BEATEN TRACK

The thought of climbing another mountain had been in my mind for some time afterwards. At first, immediately afterwards, I thought that part of my life had gone forever. And in a way, I accepted it, figuring that my legs had served me well. They'd taken me to places most people had never been, given me experiences most people had never had. For that I was grateful, and I had to console myself with positive memories. As my strength and mobility increased, though, I found myself pondering more and more. I wondered where I could go, what I could climb that would be difficult but well within the realms of possibility.

The time eventually arrived when I just had to get out of the city again. I needed a taste of nature and rang Per to see what his plans were for the next few days.

'I need to get away before I go mad,' was his response.

Neither of us really knew where we wanted to go, so we headed north. (If in doubt, always head north!) We decided on Wyperfeld National Park, in the state's north west. I'd never been there before. Per had been there as a child on a family camping trip and couldn't remember much about it. We arrived after dark, and Per set off in search of firewood while I started some water boiling on the Trangia. He was having trouble finding wood, the sparsely forested campsite having been picked clean. I watched the beacon of his torch-light scour the whole area in a huge arc around the camp. Deciding to give him a hand, I sat my torch in the netting under my chair and headed for the tree line. I didn't realise what I was doing until I had placed the first piece of wood under the chair next to the torch. I smiled to myself, the words of Stuart Tripp (a great bloke I had met recently at the Talbot) echoing through my mind: 'Mate, you are doing this too easy. You can do anything. You know that, don't you?' Stuart had lost a leg after a car accident a few years before. By the smile constantly on his face, you'd think he'd found one!

We hadn't bothered putting up a tent. Without a cloud in the sky, it would have been sacrilege to sleep in one. I lay on my back, sleeping bag half open in the warm night, gazing up at the night sky. The stars glittered like scattered jewels, so much brighter away from the bright lights of the city. It was hard to imagine these were the same stars I had lain under only six months earlier on Hinchinbrook, the contrast in circumstances immeasurable. I felt relaxed, at ease with my exposure to the open air. Revelling in my release from the confines of an enclosing structure. Finding sanctuary in the face of vulnerability. Why is it that we live our lives within sterile structures? Why have we set out to tame the world, expanding our enclosure? In doing so, we're losing our natural world — the world, I believe, that holds the key to the truth of our very existence. Laying myself open to the real world, I felt at peace with it, drifting off on a journey through the dreamscape as the campfire embers glowed softly beside me.

After a quick breakfast and the mandatory cups of coffee, we decided to 'walk' a circuit that would take us about ten kilometres through mallee heathland. The track led through an old river bed that had become a flood plain. Now, with the salinity resulting from land clearing, and the irrigation coming off the river, it was little more than a sandpit! Pushing along that sandy track was gut busting work. The sweat poured from me as I pressed forward, constantly bogged down in deep sand. Stopping to rest frequently, I took in the dry, sparse surroundings. The mallee scrub is so different from anything I had spent time in before — mostly dry grassland, with a thin covering of eucalypt. Wallabies and kangaroos grazed in the distance, bouncing away upon sighting us.

On and on I pushed, enjoying the workout and savouring the freedom. Finally reaching the gravel road, I smiled to myself, knowing I'd just covered five kilometres of difficult terrain. The boundaries in my mind began to expand; I knew now that I wouldn't be confined to the concrete footpath. *If I can do this already, who knows what is possible?*

The rest of the circuit held a few surprises of its own, taking us up and down through the hilly terrain, the road not making travel a hell of a lot easier. When we reached the car, I felt that satisfying exhaustion that you only get after a hard day's work.

As we left the park just on dusk, my mind began to wander through the possibilities that lay before me. *I could make it down to Sealers Cove in Wilson's Promontory*, I thought, my mind tracing back, trying to recall the most difficult sections of the walk. I could do some of the walks around O'Briens Crossing (a bush camp west of Melbourne which I'd been visiting since I was five or six years old), I realised. But I was looking for something bigger and better.

I reckon I could get up Cradle Mountain. Now that would be something!

Cradle Mountain rises above the central plateau in Tasmania's World Heritage area. I'd climbed it twice before. Standing at 1545 metres, it was something that would challenge me completely yet still be achievable. *I wonder . . . Could I really do it?*

The following day found us in the Grampians National Park, further south. It was turning into another hot day, and we needed to find a place to swim. Eventually we found a shaded picnic area and started out on a track cut into the hillside, the river running below. I had to jump out of the chair often, the track too steep or the obstacles too big to get over. We reached the river at a point that opened out into a small rock pool. Climbing over one rock at a time, I slowly made my way towards the water, careful not to knock my stumps on the hard rock. I still hadn't been into the water, not even a swimming pool, due to the wound in my stump. But it was as good as healed now, and it seemed fitting that my first swim be in a place like this. Having sat on the edge for a few minutes to take in my surroundings, I peeled off my clothes and stayed at the water's edge for a moment before lowering myself into the cold pool.

My skin tried to crawl back up my body, retreating from the water's icy touch. *Man, it was cold!* I slid further in, slithering over the slippery, moss covered rocks until the water rose to chest level. Taking a deep breath, I leant forward and pushed my head under, the water racing down my back as I arched to bring my head back up.

'Shit!' I gasped heavily. 'That's bloody cold!'

Per laughed from the opposite bank. He couldn't resist the temptation, though, and was soon in the river also. Like a pair of lizards, we basked in the midday sun. We would have been quite a sight, had someone come along: two blokes lying naked across the rocks, one of them with no legs!

It felt so good to be alive, to soak up the warmth of the sun, the trickle of the stream running alongside, the birds chatting away in the trees above us, going about their daily routine despite our intrusion. I listened as the wind swept gently through the trees and I knew. I knew then that I hadn't lost everything. A huge hurdle had been put in my way, along with what had seemed insurmountable obstacles. But I could get over them. Or around them. It would take just one step at a time. It would be as simple, and as difficult, as that. I would need to be patient and I would need support from people prepared to adjust to my decreased mobility. I lay there smiling as another barrier faded into oblivion, the possibilities it had prevented me from realising now spread out before me.

I am going to climb Cradle Mountain. I can do it, I know I can.

MY MISSION

I returned to Melbourne with a new lease of life, a purpose. A mission. Catching up over dinner with Daphne, I let it slip casually into the conversation.

'I'm going to climb Cradle Mountain, Daph.'

'Cradle Mountain in Tasmania?' she replied hesitantly, not quite knowing whether to be concerned or excited.

'That's the one,' I replied matter-of-factly.

'Isn't that, like, a mountain?' she asked, probably running through a list in her mind of the first signs of insanity.

'It is. But I reckon I can do it. I've gone over it in my mind, and I know I can do it.'

'When?' she asked, the hesitation in her face slowly being replaced with excitement.

'January or Feb next year,' I replied (it was now October 1997), 'while there's a good chance of fine weather.'

That was it. Now that I'd told someone, I had to do it. I started telling anyone else that asked what my plans were. I'm sure some people didn't believe me, but that was OK. It only made me more determined to pull it off.

I was going to need some new equipment. A lot of my gear had been lost or damaged on Hinchinbrook. I began writing letters to outdoor shops in Melbourne and found a sponsor in Bogong Equipment. They had the range of gear I needed. After meeting with Simon Head, the owner, I left with all the equipment I required. Mont, a company based in Canberra, supplied me with a shortened sleeping bag, undoubtedly the shortest they had ever made. (Although they were later to alter it to make it even shorter!)

I began a routine based around bar dips and chin-ups, increasing the repetitions as I grew stronger. Before long, I was doing three sets of twenty bar dips, and three sets of fifteen chin-ups, twice a day. But I needed more! I wasn't happy with my aerobic fitness, or the spare tyre I couldn't remove from around my waist. Although I had become so good on the wobble board that I could play 'wobble ball', the tyre remained. Wobble ball is a game Allison devised because she thought the wobble board had become too easy for me. It was basically a modified game of tennis, played sitting down, on the wobble board!

Everything was running according to plan. All I had to do was stay in shape in preparation for the climb. To do that, I needed to swim.

I took Brett with me to the Collingwood indoor pool one afternoon. I had no idea what was going to happen. The swim I'd had in the river with Per had only been in half a metre of water, so I still had no idea how my body would sit in the water. The first time I'd sat in a bath, I was dealt the rather humbling blow of being knocked over by the wave I'd made when I sat down as it returned from the end of the bath!

There I sat on the edge of the pool, with Brett standing by, no doubt wondering how he was going to know whether or not he needed to pull me out. Pushing myself off the edge, I dived in sideways, swimming straight to the bottom. My bum tried to rise to the surface, so I had to swim strongly to stay down there. Twisting my body around, I made for the surface. Brett stood eagerly at the side. 'How is it?' he asked.

'All right, I think,' I replied, finding it more difficult to tread water than it had been to swim under it. As I spoke, my lower body slid out from under me, rising to the surface behind me. In the process, my face was pushed down into the water, which, needless to say, gave me a bit of a surprise. Rolling over, I managed to get myself upright again.

'Well, that answers that question,' I called out to Brett, who was still wondering whether I needed rescuing or not.

'What question's that?' he asked.

'Whether my legs used to float or not,' I replied.

I felt like I was trying to balance on a balloon underwater, having to keep my weight over it to stop it from tipping me off as it made its way to the surface. Your legs act as a kind of ballast in the water; without any, I constantly had to keep myself over my lower body.

I began swimming seriously in the hydrotherapy pool at the Talbot. Because it was so small, I couldn't do proper laps in it. Unable to 'kick' off the wall, I came to a standstill at the end of each lap and completely lost all momentum. Swimming laps in a *fifty* metre pool is difficult for this reason; in the *ten* metres available at the Royal Talbot, it was out of the question. The solution was to attach a rubber line to a railing at the end of the pool, and tie it to a buoyancy belt around my waist. It felt pretty strange thrashing away in the one spot while people walked up and down the pool, but I could feel it doing me good!

Before long, I could swim for half an hour each session, at a steady pace without stopping. I began to feel a hell of a lot fitter, and started swimming regularly with Deirdre McEwan, a Kiwi friend I'd first met at the train station in Munich. We swam as often as we could, under the summer sun in the 50 metre outdoor pool in Fitzroy. This gave me great satisfaction, in that, once out of my chair and in the pool, I could hold my own with the other swimmers — in the water, I felt far from disabled.

WALKING

With my legs now healed, it was time to recommence prosthetic training. Whereas, before, I'd been restricted to walking within the parallel bars, it was now time to move outside them. Standing at the end of the bars, I took hold of the walking frame in front of me and stepped forward. Helen Connor and Mark McDonald, my new physios, stood either side of me, encouraging me on as I stepped forward slowly, making my way across the room. When I reached a bed on the other side, I turned around and sat down carefully.

Sitting down and standing up were, and still are, the two most difficult aspects of walking for me. As my knees give me support only when they are extended, locking into place, they need to be 'broken' for me to sit. And I need to break them carefully because, once they're broken, they offer no support at all. If I don't take all my weight through my arms, I'm sent straight back down into my chair much harder than I'd prefer, or straight to the ground!

Twice a day, in between my rigorous training and stretching sessions, I'd practise walking. Some days, if I couldn't get the legs to fit properly, I would have to take them off after walking a few steps, the pain unbearable. My legs changed shape constantly, despite the elastic sleeves called 'shrinkers' that I wore. These are used to keep the stumps to a uniform volume but they weren't doing a very good job in my case. As a result, sometimes I just couldn't get into the sockets of my legs correctly, which made walking impossible.

As time progressed, I moved on to walking-sticks, and could now walk up and down the corridor outside the gym. The most important milestone for me, though, was walking around the perimeter of the building. Up the steep hill outside the gym I struggled, one step at a time, amazed at how much effort it took to get to the top. Walking around to the front of the building, I stepped through the main entrance and up to the front counter. The girls behind the desk had never seen me out of a wheelchair, and they smiled in admiration. It felt so good to stand at the counter, looking over the desk at them instead of up at them. After a quick chat, I continued on down the corridor to the lift, taking it down to the second floor and walking back to the amputee gym. I slumped into my chair, exhausted. There I began the arduous task of taking my legs off, quickly removing the uncomfortable Neoprene belt from around my waist. I'd done it. I had walked around the block! My legs were stiff and sore, but it didn't matter. At least I knew I could do it.

I reached an unconscious decision after that walk. I knew what I could achieve now and felt satisfied with that. I realised that my real goal was in getting to the top of the mountain, and that didn't involve these legs. I figured I could come back to them later. From that moment, I still walked in my legs every day until I left hospital but concentrated mainly on my training for Cradle.

When I did finally leave the Royal Talbot, I used the legs only once more before heading down to Tasmania. I wanted to show Mum and Dad what I had achieved, so I took my legs along to visit them one afternoon. It felt incredible sitting in the backyard, pulling each leg on, one at a time. It had been one thing to walk around the hospital, but now I was at home, walking again in the place where I'd first learnt to walk as a child. I stood cautiously, adjusted my belt, then stepped carefully across the uneven pink and grey paving stones outside the back door. Once on the concrete driveway, I felt much safer. I could sense Mum and Dad watching me and I imagined how they must have felt.

Looking over to them, I called, 'So. What do you reckon?'

Dad, standing now, walked towards me, reaching out.

'Mate . . . ,' his voice breaking. 'I've wanted to do this for such a long time,' he cried, his face against mine as we held each other.

Tears streamed down my face. 'I love you, Dad.'

ROCKY MOUNTAINS

I first left Australia in June 1990, flying to Los Angeles with four mates. Doug (Dig), Dirk (Dirty) and Pete had been talking about going over for quite a while. We were all into hot cars (and bikes in Dig's case) and parts were dirt cheap in the States at that stage. Dave wasn't really interested in the car side of things. He just wanted to see a bit of the States and have a good time. I decided one night that I should join them — not so much for the shopping, although I did end up buying a heap of stuff I never used.

I felt like I needed a change. I wasn't really happy with my life and where I was headed. I had a well-paid job in the engineering department with the Gas & Fuel Corporation, designing metering systems for commercial and industrial consumers. But I didn't enjoy being stuck in an office all day, wearing the collar and tie. As I joined the other sheep on the train every morning and night, I knew there had to be more to life than this; at least, I hoped there was. I was living the life of the 'weekend warrior', living for Friday night and drinking my way through the weekend. Only to start the cycle all over again each Monday morning.

I decided to join the guys on their trip to the States, then travel on afterwards, see a bit of the world. I don't believe in sitting around waiting for things to happen. I wanted to get out there and see what sort of a life I could create for myself.

I put in an application for twelve months' leave without pay, which was a common practice in the public service in those days. It was rejected, so I applied for six months. When that was rejected, I arranged a meeting with my supervisor. He offered me six weeks, my accrued annual leave.

'Forget it, I'm out of here,' I replied without hesitation, and handed in my resignation.

Some of my colleagues tried to talk me out of my decision, claiming I should at least stay for another two years to receive my long service leave.

'Yeah, right! I'm not looking forward to being here for another two weeks, let alone two years!' I looked around the building: I was surrounded by people that had been playing this game for, in some cases, 20 or 30 years.

Look at them. Do you really want to be like that?

Not everyone responded negatively to my quitting. Some of my closer workmates confided to me, 'I wish I had done that when I was your age. It's too late for me now,' which I agreed with at the time, but don't any more.

For two months, we partied our way across the States, travelling south-east from Los Angeles, through Arizona, across to Georgia and New Orleans, then north-west up through South Dakota to Colorado. By the time we reached Yellowstone National Park, I needed a break. After two months of being stuck in the car with the same guys, I had to get out. I made a deal with Dig and Dirty (Pete and Dave had gone home by this stage) for them to do their thing around the park while I took off into the hills for a few days.

Inside the park office, I bought a map of the area and with the help of the ranger on duty, selected a three-day walk into the Rocky Mountains. I organised my food, said goodbye to Dig and Dirty, and took off. It felt so good to be getting some exercise, out in the fresh air with blue sky stretching above me.

The track took me through a lightly wooded valley, the rugged peaks of the Rockies stretching out before me. Having travelled less than five kilometres from the road, I approached with curiosity what looked like a dead animal on the side of the track. *Jesus! That thing looks like it's been chewed up and spat out,* I thought to myself, realising immediately why. It had been! There are bears in Yellowstone National Park. I had been well aware of that when I left, and had run through, in my mind, all the precautions to take. But, hell, I hadn't expected to come across something like this! Already!

I stepped back onto the track, eyes scanning the tree line for any sign of movement. Seeing nothing, I quickly moved on, constantly checking in every direction, my heart trying to jump out of my chest.

From that moment on, I stayed constantly on full alert. I'd never had to worry about anything more than snakes in the bush before (well, maybe mosquitoes and leeches) — but bears? This was an entirely new playing field.

After setting up camp that night, I cooked dinner quickly. Eating in the firelight, I felt like a crow on a roadside carcass, ready to leap up and abandon my meal at a second's notice. I froze solid as I thought I heard movement in the darkness. Then *craaack* came the sound of something big moving through the trees directly in front of me! Jumping to my feet, and backwards at the same time, I held my breath, my chest pounding. With eyes like dinner plates, neck craned forward, I peered into the night. My body reacted with instinct, twisting to face the other way, ready to run. I swung around behind me, scanning the trees, looking for one to climb. *Don't run! Remember, you're not supposed to run!*

Snap! I swung around quickly, back to face the sound. *Shit! What is it? Please don't come any closer.*

Snap! Crack! A twig snapped and branches rustled as it began moving, circling the fire. I slowly backed away, moving with it, keeping the fire between us, constantly glancing over my shoulder, looking for the closest tree. I felt like I was still holding my breath, tensing my chest to stay quiet. Staring into the dark where the noise had come from, I waited for a signal to send me running for the tree. *I know I'm not supposed to, but if that bear comes for me, I'm following my instincts and running like hell!*

For what seemed an eternity, I held off from making a move, until... *Am I imagining things, or is it moving away?* I strained my ears to listen. Sure enough, it headed away from me now, until the sounds of its movement faded into the distance.

Certain that whatever it was; bear, moose or something else, it was gone, for now, I sprang into action, the adrenaline surging through me. All the food, including my half-eaten dinner, went straight into a bag and into my pack. I had already thrown a rope over a high branch away from my tent and now I quickly tied my pack to it. I had begun hoisting it up when I remembered something I'd read the previous day. Something about a bear being able to detect the smell of food in your clothes after you've cooked in them. *Shit!* I wasn't taking any chances. I stripped off and stuffed my clothes into the pack. Naked, I hoisted my pack into the tree, tied it off and scampered into the tent.

I lay absolutely still, my heart skipping a beat with every sound outside. I felt so scared, so vulnerable. For the first time, I felt what it was like to be on a lower rung of the food chain, felt the fear that man must have felt for thousands of years as he lay huddled in caves, or a grass hut on the savannah, trying to keep out of reach of animals that wanted to kill him to survive. Turning the clock back to a time before we had conquered all our predators, I felt what it was like to be hunted, to be a true part of nature, without the protection, without the privileges we now take for granted.

TO SURF, OR NOT TO SURF . . .

Using the fit ball and the wobble board for balancing practice at the Talbot had given me an idea. The time finally came for me to try it out.

Deirdre had shown no hesitation when I mentioned heading down to the coast — she had jumped at the chance to avoid study for a few days. Now, the sun beat down from a clear blue sky, hot summer air lashing our faces through the open windows as we sped down the highway towards the Great Ocean Road.

I wanted to test my buoyancy in salt water, to see how I would handle the waves that just aren't available in your average city pool. But most of all, I wanted to surf. I felt like I was surfing whenever I sat on that ball at the Talbot; the time had come to try the real thing. I had borrowed a boogie board from Stuart Tripp and couldn't wait to get it in the water.

As we pulled in to the car park at Point Roadknight beach, Anglesea, the sea before us couldn't have looked more perfect. Crystal clear water with gentle one-metre waves lay spread out before us. The concrete ramp straight into the water made it easy for me to get in, allowing me to wheel right down to the water's edge. I parked the chair, shuffling the remaining distance on my bum into the water that was lapping at the ramp. The swell threatened to unbalance me, so I leant forward in 30 centimetres of water and lunged forward.

The cold water brought every pore of my skin to life, invigorating me instantly. I swam out into deeper water, then just floated, rising and falling with the swell. Swimming in the ocean had always been one of my favourite things, one of life's simplest pleasures. Not long ago, I thought I'd lost it forever. The feeling, now, of claiming back another part of my life was incredible. I tried catching a few waves, body surfing. It was to no avail, the sea being too flat in the partly sheltered bay. *Never mind. We've got all day.*

Further along the coast, we stopped at Eastern View, a beach I used to come to as a kid with Mum and Dad. The surf was much bigger here, and the beach almost empty. I reached into the back of the car and pulled out the boogie board, which Deirdre carried down to the beach while I nearly busted my gut pushing through the sand. I'd let my tyres right down, but I still had to give it everything I had to get over the dune onto harder sand. I pushed myself to just short of the water's edge, then jumped out, dragging the boogie board behind me by the ankle strap (*Mmmm. A lot of good that's going to do me!*).

The bigger, stronger waves made it very difficult even to get into the water. The first one knocked me straight over; so did the second, as soon as I had got back up again. I struggled onto my stomach and started swimming in the shallow water, but got pulled back as the next wave caught hold of the board. I must have looked pretty funny, floundering around like a pissed dugong in thirty centimetres of water! After what seemed an eternity, I reached deeper water, only to be sent back by the next wave as it broke right in front of me. *Shit!*

I started again, this time regaining ground quickly, working out a way to get through the breakers. I had to hug the board as the waves hit me. I couldn't paddle through them as I used to. Every time I tried, the board slid out from underneath me. Once outside the breaking waves, I just lay forward on the board to rest. *This is bloody hard work!*

As I waited for the right wave, I tried to get myself balanced on the board, but it kept shooting out from under me. *This is bloody ridiculous! I need some wax or something.* I just could not get enough grip. Spotting a decent wave behind me, I went to paddle forward but came straight off as soon as it hit me. I tumbled through with the wave, getting completely trashed. I came up gasping for air in the foam and decided I'd had enough. I dragged myself up the beach, disappointed, but not shattered. I knew that, with some grip on the board, I could do better.

As my swimming improved, I started thinking more and more of an ocean race I'd swum about ten years before — the 'Pier to Pub' swim at Lorne, two hours west of Melbourne on the Great Ocean Road. I decided that, as soon as I could swim the race distance of 1.2 kilometres, I'd sign myself up for it. It wasn't long before I'd achieved that goal, swimming 1.6 kilometres just to make sure. Deirdre was keen to swim it too, so we began training in earnest.

I swam the race on January 10th 1998 in 23 minutes and one second, faster than I'd swum it in 1987! I finished 473rd in my age group, leaving 259 competitors to deal with the fact that they'd been beaten by a bloke with no legs! I felt on top of the world, for the first time proving that my disability would not hold me back. In the water, it didn't matter that I had no legs. Nobody would have known. Until I got to the shoreline that is.

As the other swimmers alongside me stood up in the shallow water and began running towards the beach, I kept swimming, pulling myself along the sandy bottom when the water became too shallow to swim in. Waves breaking over me, I sat up in the water and began shuffling up the beach on my arse. Per spotted me and came to my aid with the wheelchair. The first time I swung myself up to get in it, my arms gave way, and I crashed down heavily into the sand. The second time, I made it and began pushing as hard as I could towards the finish line. I felt the stares of people watching me, but concentrated totally on getting to the finish line. As the sand became softer where it had been churned up by the swimmers funnelling in to the finishing flags, I had to get out of the chair again. I crossed the finish line on my bum, to cheers of support from the crowd. I had reclaimed another part of my life.

Cradle Mountain couldn't come along fast enough. I was hungry for it.

The following day found a group of us, all nursing horrendous hangovers, back at Eastern View Beach. I had a block of surfboard wax with me this time and was determined to redeem myself. Spurred on by Bunyip (Andrew Bryant, a good friend of mine on the Sunshine Coast), who has a backward bodysurfing style that has to be seen to be believed, I caught three decent waves. Riding them in to shore, I felt like the first person ever to do so.

CRADLE MOUNTAIN

It was with a sense of destiny that I drove into Cradle Valley that cold Thursday afternoon. Low cloud shrouded the peaks, misty rain forming a soft haze that created an otherworldly atmosphere. In my car with me were Cate Weate and Michael Croll. I'd spent a lot of time with Cate in the Tarkine and felt good about having her with me on this trip. I had driven across with Michael (whom I'd met through Christine and Ebi) from his home in the north-east, picking Cate up in Launceston. Lisa and Per had wanted to see more of Tasmania since visiting me in Weldborough. Keen to climb the mountain with me, they had come across on the same ferry. Unfortunately, they would have to leave early due to work commitments. They pulled in behind us as we reached the Parks office.

Wheeling into the building, I felt suddenly confronted by my surroundings. The whole building was set up for bushwalkers, providing information and recommending walks. I couldn't help thinking that people might be looking at me, wondering what I was doing here. With some hesitation, I wheeled up to the counter where a ranger stood, his badge saying 'Peter'.

'G'day mate. I've got a hut booked under the name of Macdonald, for tonight'.

'You must be the bloke that's going to climb the mountain, hey?' he replied.

I almost blushed with relief. For some reason I thought that, even now, people might laugh when I mentioned my intentions. That they might give me that look that says 'Oh, the poor thing. He thinks he can climb a mountain. Isn't that terrible!' I felt like a coiled spring. Like a jack in the box just waiting to burst out and surprise everyone. Projecting the stereotypical image of the helpless cripple just by being in a wheelchair, people had no idea of what I was capable of. I gained strength from his positive response.

'I surely am,' I replied confidently, smiling.

'That's going to be pretty impressive if you get up there, mate. I've been around in my time, seen some amazing things. If you can get up there, and can tell me what's up there when you get back, I'll make up one of our new certificates for you,' he said, brimming with enthusiasm.

'I'll get up there. Don't you worry about that,' I replied. 'It would make things easier if the weather cleared up a bit, though.'

Though still technically summer, Tassie runs to its own schedule. Storms had been lashing the state over the previous few days, and although the wind had died down somewhat, it remained bitterly cold. Up on the plateau, it would be colder still.

Leaving ranger Peter, we got back into the cars and drove the winding road through the valley to Waldheim. Gustav Weindorfer had built the first hut here in 1912. He was a man who had recognised the beauty of being in the wild, gaining spiritual rejuvenation through the wilderness. I wondered what he would think if he could see his valley now. His dream of Cradle Mountain being 'a national park for the people' had certainly come to fruition.

The rain had become heavier as we pulled up outside the hut. Moving inside quickly, Per set about lighting a fire. He and Lisa were freezing, the notorious Tasmanian weather having taken them totally by surprise.

'I'd hate to see you here in winter!' I joked, having a go at them.

We ate a huge bowl of pasta each and had settled back to relax when there was a knock at the door. Through it walked Eddie Storace, complete with cask of port!

'Eddie! Me old mate!'

'Wazza! You old bastard!' he greeted me warmly in return.

Eddie and I had met through our involvement in the Tarkine campaign and I'd spent a lot of time with him and his partner Helen at their home in Sisters Beach. I'd been in the bush with Eddie only once, but what a trip it had been! The pair of us, with Kai and Bo, had taken four days to cut a track through 15 kilometres of wilderness carrying 20 kilos of rapid-set concrete (it's a long story!) ... and Eddie had thought he'd just been invited on a casual bushwalk!

I hadn't seen Eddie since leaving Tassie nearly two years earlier, which meant he hadn't seen me since the accident. It always feels weird seeing people again now. I go through the same feelings of awkwardness every time I meet an old friend who hasn't seen me since the accident, feeling apprehensive within myself as to how people are going to respond to me, being fully aware of the shock it must be to see someone so physically changed. Thankfully, he, like most others, quickly realised something that had struck me too: that, hey, it's still me. I'm just two feet shorter, both literally and in height.

What's happened to the film crew? I wondered. The plan was to meet us either here or at the Cradle Mountain lodge. We were running late, but we still had to get ourselves organised; they knew where to find us and could do so at a later stage. When we hadn't heard from them by 8.00pm, I was starting to fear the worst. *Could they have been called away on another job? Surely they'd have let us know. But then again, this is the media were talking about.*

I tried not to think about it too much, deciding that they'd turn up in the morning if they were still in the state. I finished packing the rest of my gear. All the food had been measured out and allocated to individual packs. We'd double-checked our stoves and first aid gear. We were ready to go.

Sliding into my sleeping bag, my mind raced at the thought of the next day's journey, I asked myself *What are you getting yourself into here? Do you really know what you're doing?* All of these doubts crashed around in my head against the positive belief that I was ready; that it was now or never; that I knew I could do it. So juggling, I drifted off to sleep.

The day began slowly — I felt so snug in my sleeping bag that I refused to admit I was awake, prolonging the inevitability of facing the brisk Tasmanian morning. It seemed too early to get up yet, and I let myself believe this for a while until I began thinking of the day ahead. Then I felt a sense of urgency. Out of the bag and dressing quickly, I roused the others. They'd all been lying there like myself, each of us waiting till the other made a move first.

'C'mon, get up!' I called out in mock order. 'Let's get amongst it!'

Through the cabin window I was greeted with a rather grim looking day, shrouded in low cloud. This was pretty typical of early morning in this part of Tassie, but we had the added unwelcome element of steady drizzling rain. Early morning cloud is often dispersed as soon as the mid-morning sun touches it, but this drizzle could easily stay with us all day.

I had known all along that, if it were going to rain, it would be nice if it rained on the first day, rather than the second. I really needed fine weather for the summit attempt, as any rain would make the quartzite boulders very slippery. Bad weather below would make the trip uncomfortable, possibly even miserable, but wouldn't stop me from continuing. I'd decided earlier that if we did strike bad weather up at Kitchen Hut, at the foot of the mountain, I would have to wait it out there. It would then be in the lap of the gods as to whether I made it to the top or not. I could only wait as long as those helping me were prepared to stay.

As soon as we'd had breakfast, I asked Lisa if she could drive back to the Cradle Mountain lodge to try to find the film crew. The rest of us moved the vehicles down to the car park then started making the last minute adjustments to our packs. Gore-Tex clad day-trippers eyed me suspiciously, surely wondering what the hell I was up to.

My pack lay under the seat of my wheelchair, strapped in to the frame. I had fixed it underneath weeks before, giving me a chance to get used to the extra weight. Inside was my sleeping bag, therma-rest mat, all my clothing, a torch . . . Basically, everything except my stove, tent and food.

I pushed up and down the pot-holed gravel road, trying to keep moving to stay warm. Rolling downhill, I was surprised at how tightly I had to grip the push-rim to keep control of the chair. My hands were freezing already and we hadn't even got onto the track! I wondered how I would go when I struck a tough stretch of track, whether I could push through it with my hands like this.

It was time to sign our intentions into the logbook. This was located in a little wooden shelter, partially sided, with a roof offering minimal but much appreciated protection from the bitter wind. I held my hands up to my mouth and cupped them together, blowing warm air over them, rubbed them together, then blew on them again. I had to get them warm before I could manage to write anything. As I turned from signing off my entry, Lisa stepped into view, heading my way with a couple of guys looking very much like a film crew. *Excellent.*

I wheeled over to greet them. 'How is it going, guys? I thought we must have lost you.'

'So did we. When we hadn't heard from you by 9.00pm last night, we thought the whole thing might have been called off,' one of them answered, sounding a bit put out that we hadn't chased him up then.

'No chance of that mate,' I replied. 'We got here a bit later than expected and thought, well, you guys know where we are. We'll let you come to us. Anyway mate, I'm Warren Macdonald. You must be Nick?'

'Sorry, yes. Nick Coe. And this is Simon, our sound man.' He introduced the guy with the furry microphone.

With the introductions over, I was keen to get moving, happy now that things were falling into place.

'Ready when you are,' Nick replied. He was wearing a pair of denim jeans, which told me he hadn't done a lot of bushwalking before. I didn't envy him really. He was going to be pretty uncomfortable in those if this drizzle kept up.

I wheeled back up the road to the beginning of the eighty kilometre overland track. It had been two years since I was last here, on a day trip to the summit of Cradle. I'd been standing on two legs that day. Legs that I'd *had* only 10 months before.

OK. You can do this. Let's go!

I put myself into a mono and began descending the steep track. With my seat belt pulled tight, I felt secure, but the track was extremely slippery. Leaning right back, I came to a series of steps leading on to the first stretch of duckboard. (Duckboard is the walkway — usually wooden — that is built to protect fragile areas from the damaging effects of large numbers of hikers.) I dropped down these steps one by one, not having counted on bouncing so much each time I landed. With the track sloping to the left, each time I bounced I landed further across until finally, with nowhere else to go, I bounced straight off the side! The duckboard was only 45 centimetres above the ground, so I didn't have far to fall. I would have liked to have seen the looks on the faces of the others, though — especially the film crew.

My laughter reassured everyone that I was OK. *So this is going to be more interesting than I thought!*

My seat belt had held me into the chair, and I'd begun to wonder whether that was a good thing or not. Undoing it, I slid out of the chair and climbed back onto the boards. There would be so many unknown factors on this trip. I had been able to plan only so far, not being able to find anyone who had done any off-road work in a wheelchair before. It would be a case of tackling each new problem as it arose and working out a way around it.

Strapped back into my chair, I started again. I soon came to a drop that I knew was too big. I'd fall out of my chair for sure if I attempted it. Undoing my seat belt, I climbed out and shuffled around it on my hands and bum, then back into the chair again until the next obstacle arose. Slowly, ever so slowly, we crossed the plain that way, with me continuously in and out of the chair. Hooded figures stood patiently behind me as the cold wind swept misty rain across the plain.

Nobody said much. I think everybody had begun to realise privately the enormity of what we had set out to achieve. I wondered what they thought, if they could begin to imagine what this must be like for me. For someone who had been at his best when walking, now reduced to this. Shuffling along the ground like some kind of sideshow freak. I pushed the negative thoughts to the back of my mind, telling myself, *One step at a time. That's all you have to do.*

Stopping often to rest, I took in the landscape around me. This was such a beautiful place. A lot of Tasmanians discounted this place because of what it had become: a tourist destination. It certainly was that, but not without good reason; and that reason was why I was here, tourists or no tourists.

After an hour of duckboard we began climbing the first of the moraines, following alongside and above Crater Creek before entering the first section of rainforest. Myrtle and sassafras formed a canopy over our heads as the forest around us became covered in a blanket of moss. The damp smells of the forest hung in the very air. This is what I'd come here for. This is why I'd been so enchanted with Tassie since first arriving: the timelessness, the almost magical feeling evoked by being in a place like this.

Climbing the pine staircase, I leaned forward over each step before swinging my body up and onto the next. I felt strong, actually preferring these steeper sections as I felt I was really achieving something in gaining height, rather than just shuffling along the ground. Climbing was what I had trained for.

Onwards and upwards we continued before I heard the excited voices up ahead. I knew they could see the lake now, but not just the lake. From below, we couldn't actually see any of the major mountains; they remained hidden behind the veil of mist and rain. I knew what it was that had them going. They'd just come face to face with the escarpment of Marion's Lookout. A seemingly sheer wall rising 200 metres above the surface of Crater Lake takes you onto the plateau above. I think that was the first moment that Lisa actually realised the extent of this trip. That this was in fact a mountain (as Daphne had pointed out) and not just a sloping hill.

'How do we get up there?' she asked.

'See to the left there,' I pointed. 'The track zigzagging up the face?'

'Yeah?' she replied hesitantly, almost in disbelief.

'That's where we're going. That track takes us onto the top of the plateau,' I answered confidently, butterflies rising in my stomach at the sight. The climb now seemed five times higher than I recalled from my last visit here.

The news crew did a quick interview with me beside the lake before leaving us for the day, the plan being for them to return to the comfort of the lodge, then catch up with us again in the morning at

Kitchen Hut. We wished them well, then huddled into Gustav's old boat shed on the lake shore for some lunch. Trangias boiled away as we made the first of a number of coffees — accompanied by large quantities of chocolate, of course!

I felt strong physically; but extremely vulnerable at the same time, sitting in a small three-sided shack, hours away from civilisation, with no legs. There was no quick escape route for me and I think that's what played on my mind more than anything. The thought that if anything did go wrong, I'd have to rely on others to get me out. I'd never experienced that before Hinchinbrook. I wasn't in a hurry to experience it again.

Leaving the relative security of the hut, we made our way around the lake, climbing gently towards the escarpment. I hopped out of the chair. Per, Michael and Eddie disassembled it for the ascent. Carrying it would be no easy task for them, as the track was mainly loose scree. It would be difficult walking at the best of times, let alone shouldering a pack whilst carrying a wheelchair!

All I could concentrate on was the step directly in front of me cut into the mountainside and reinforced with pine, each one being a new hurdle to overcome. Each step had to be considered a new obstacle. Some, I had to lift my bum up onto as I held the sides, bracing with my forearms. Others were too steep to be negotiated that way, and I had to slide up on my chest before sitting up. I had a feeling that, if I did fall backwards, I wouldn't be able to stop myself from tumbling, without legs. I hadn't proven this theory yet, and was in no big hurry to, either. I moved carefully, one step at a time up the steep slope until finally, after an hour or so, I reached the top. There in front of me, its jagged lines cut out of the horizon, stood my destination.

'Wogsy! That's huge!' Lisa exclaimed.

'It is, isn't it. Check it out!' I replied, happy to just sit and look at it for a while. Then, breaking my silence: 'All right. Kitchen Hut's not far from here. We'd better keep moving.'

Moving across the plateau was made easier by the fact that I could see the mountain most of the time. The track between Marion's Lookout and Kitchen Hut rolled over a gentle arc, occasionally cut by creeks running down towards the lakes below. Each time the track dipped down into one of these creeks, I lost sight of the hut, taking away my urgency to keep moving. That said, at some points when I *could* see the hut, I felt I wasn't making any progress at all. My wrists were aching from taking most of the strain. I alternated between moving on my palms, which was harder on my wrists, and using my knuckles in a clenched fist. This was easier on my wrists, but very hard on my knuckles, especially when moving over scree. My forearms burnt also with each forward step, taking my full weight as I swung my body over them.

The sun sank lower as I approached Kitchen Hut, the last 100 metres seeming to take forever. My ambling into the camp drew a chorus of whoops and yelps. Eddie hugged me fiercely: 'Wazza! Mate!'

Cate stood behind me, hugging me tight. 'You're a legend, Waz.' I felt like I'd won the first half of a marathon.

I made it! I've made it to Kitchen Hut!

It was now 6:00pm. It had taken us all day to get here but we had made it. I was so glad to see everyone sharing my excitement. I still hadn't gotten used to the idea of people having to stop and wait for me every five minutes; it made me feel very uncomfortable. Sitting with my back against the hut on a slab of stone, I looked up at the peak before me, clouds partly obscuring it.

It had taken me a long time after the accident to dare to *dream* of climbing a mountain like this again. I wrestled with it for weeks, even once I'd decided within myself, I was scared to tell anyone of my plan for fear of being accused of aiming too high. I didn't want to take the risk of people feeling sorry for me, getting my hopes up on some ridiculous idea of climbing a mountain, with no legs! It was only when I started to feel strong and spent some time in the bush again that I knew I could do it, knew I could tell people without having to back down.

Sitting just inside the hut's doorway, I watched the shadows creep across the face of the mountain in front of me, growing longer before my eyes. Black clouds were gathering in the east, but you could never really tell what the weather might do up here. Inexperienced walkers still get caught out on Cradle, even in the middle of summer. There have been a number of deaths up there over the years, mostly from people underestimating the mountain's changeable weather and being unprepared for the worst.

With the sun sinking into the horizon, I sat back and rested while the others prepared the evening meal. No sooner had we eaten than my sleeping bag beckoned me. It had been such a long day. My aching body needed some rest, my mind still racing at what I had achieved. At what lay ahead.

As I lay in my sleeping bag on the wooden floor, my legs just wouldn't warm up. There was too much air space in the bag where my legs used to be, making it difficult to retain my body heat. Using a length of webbing, I tied the end of the bag off, effectively reducing its size, I warmed up in no time.

Drifting off to sleep I felt like I'd regained something that day, something I'd prided myself on before the accident. The ability to take myself out of my comfort zone and to learn from the experience. Throughout the day now passing, I'd been well within my comfort zone as I *used* to know it. But I had proved that, even though I'd been cut down physically, I could still take myself out, not just to the new frontiers that I faced every day, but to some old ones as well. It was with that thought that I fell asleep, totally at peace with myself for one of the few times in my life.

The cold kept us snuggled in our bags again the following morning. I'd never really been one of those up-at-the-crack-of-dawn types of hiker. The type that gives everybody the shits in communal huts by stomping around in heavy boots at 5.00am. I prefer a more leisurely start to the day.

Hearing Cate stir beside me, I knew it was time to face the day. It couldn't have been more than four or five degrees Celsius — bloody freezing! I shuffled out of my bag quickly and dressed in all the clothes I had with me. Opening the door of the hut presented me with a glorious sight: a clear blue sky with not a cloud in sight!

The gods are smiling on us!

THE SUMMIT

We were all in such high spirits. So much hinged on the weather this day and it looked like we were going to be in luck. If the weather turned bad, it would mean having to postpone any summit attempt until it cleared. At best, we could afford to be holed up for a day, possibly two. I couldn't expect the others to stay any longer than that, and I couldn't stay here alone.

Sitting outside the hut in the morning sun, two figures appeared across the plateau, making their way towards us. One of them the unmistakable form of Brian Hall, the other, his wife Val.

It felt so good to see Brian again, especially in this setting. This is how he had first come to know me: in the outdoors, at my best. And that was how he was seeing me again now. I'd thought I might feel weakened seeing Brian, that he might have felt sorry for me seeing me as I am now. But, thankfully, I was wrong. He'd respected me as a bush-walker, seeing that this was something I did well. Seeing him now, like this, feeling his admiration for me in having got here, made me feel so much stronger. He has that quality, to bring out the best in people. He and Val had taken the weekend off to see me reach the top.

As we reacquainted ourselves again, Lisa and Per prepared them-selves for their trip to the top. They were booked on the 4.00pm ferry from Devonport back to Melbourne that afternoon. They would have to leave now if they were to make the summit in time. I wished them luck as they made their way to the mountain's base.

Ten minutes later, another two figures approached from Marion's Lookout. This time it was Meagan Doherty, a reporter from the *Examiner*, a Tasmanian newspaper based in Launceston. She'd done a story on my involvement in the Tarkine campaign when I'd first returned to Tassie after my accident. I'd been impressed with the results after having been savaged by the Tasmanian media during Tarkine times. With her was Jeremy Smith, photographer, who we discovered later was quite an experienced climber.

No sooner had we done all the introductions than another group appeared, with two smaller members out in front, running towards us: Ebi and Ian, with their respective sons Seppi and Kieran. This was the first time on Cradle Mountain for all of them. Again a reunion atmosphere took over, but not for long. We had to get moving. The time was nigh, and I had a job to do.

Looking up at the mountain once more, bathed in sunlight, I low-ered my head and made my first shuffle forward over the earthen track. In places the track cut through what would normally be shin deep alpine heath. I had to turn and twist, at times dragging myself through it. As I climbed the steadily steepening track, earth gave way to what is known as 'talus' and 'scree' — rock fragments that have crumbled off the mountain, piling up below (talus is usually big enough to be used as stepping stones; scree ranges from small to large pebbles). I was forced to lift my bum higher to clear the rough ground. Onwards and onwards we climbed, eventually stopping at a small spring for a scroggin break (scroggin is high energy food, usually dried fruit and nuts).

The day had a fairly relaxed atmosphere about it. Although I found the climbing very demanding physically, I had total confidence that I was going to make it, which kept me calm and relaxed mentally. As the hours passed we found ourselves bathed in the sunshine of a perfect summer's day: not so hot as to make it unbearable, but not a cloud in the sky all the same. I chatted with different people as we climbed, with Brian about what other course members were doing with themselves these days, about what I was doing in Melbourne now that my rehabilitation was over.

Eventually the scree gave way to huge blocks of dolerite looming above me and I had to lie on my stomach to drag myself up and over each piece at a time. Huge columns towered above me, the remnants of which made up the talus and scree below, stating their instability. As I gained height, the climbing became steeper, until eventually it got too steep for me to climb without great risk of tumbling backwards. Since I still didn't know how I would stop myself if I did tumble back, it was about time to set up the first pitch of technical climbing.

Brian and Jeremy set up a top rope–bottom belay system, fixing a sling around a large boulder up above, while I put on my harness. As I got the OK to climb, and began edging my way up the slab, a sudden uneasiness crept into me, something I had successfully avoided until now.

My weight is pulling on this rock. If it comes loose, I'm underneath it.

The realisation shook me to the bone. I cringed deep within myself, momentarily reliving the experience, feeling the rock give way in my mind.

No, it couldn't! It couldn't happen again, could it?

I tried to reassure myself that it wasn't possible. That fate just could not be so cruel.

If it does come down, then so be it. It was just never meant to be.

I was actually angry at the thought, the possibility that some God above could be so cruel as to let another rock fall on me like this. I was almost issuing a challenge: *Go on, you wouldn't dare! Even you couldn't be so cruel.*

I reached for an edge and, once found, used it to pull myself up with one arm while I worked the other beneath me to mantle myself forward. Then, lying flat on my stomach, I reached up to repeat the move, inching my way up towards the top of the boulder. At the top, I looked over the edge to see a huge gap between myself and the next slab. *Shit, this is going to be interesting.*

I carefully got my hands into position, then lowered my body down between the two slabs of rock, feeling so soft and vulnerable between the hard, rough stone. Once down in the gap, I began the climb up the face of the next boulder. And so it went for the next three hours before we reached the amphitheatre just below the summit.

Running out of daylight now, it was clear that we needed to get some gear up here for a night on the summit. We couldn't possibly make it up and down in the day as planned. Ebi, Ian, Eddie and Michael volunteered to do a dash back down to the hut.

Gathering all the available water bags, they took off, at great speed, hoping to make it back in time for my arrival at the summit. I kept moving, arriving in the amphitheatre I knew was close to the top. It was like a huge hollow in the mountaintop, and we actually had to descend into it, then traverse above the gorge it fell into, before climbing steeply onto the main summit plateau.

It was damp in there. Very little sun penetrates into the recesses on the mountaintop and a community of different plants live up there in the shadows. On both my previous visits there had been a patch of snow still hiding in the shadows. In the middle of summer!

The view from this saddle was spectacular, giving us our first lookout to the east, across to the Walls of Jerusalem and beyond, over seemingly endless rugged peaks, deep gorges and lakes. My spirit soared at the sight and I began to feel the adrenaline course through my veins.

I'm almost there! I'm going to make it!

I was now at the section I had remembered as being the most likely to give me trouble. The climb out of the amphitheatre involved five to six metres of almost vertical rock. One section of roughly two metres was slightly overhung, enough for some members of our party to remove their packs before attempting it. Jeremy set up this last pitch, belaying from below, with Brian encouraging me on from above. Not that I needed any encouragement now, I was so close to the top.

Hauling myself up I still felt strong, even stronger as I sensed my goal to be so close. When I reached the overhang, I was forced to climb the rope, reaching the top and scraping over the edge on my stomach. Brian was going off.

'Wazza! You're there, son!'

I untied from my harness and just sat at the edge, taking in the spectacular scenery, savouring the exhilarating feeling of being on a mountain again, my senses reeling with adrenaline and the sheer emotion of what I'd been through to get here, how I never thought I'd get here again. Looking down onto the track far below, it was hard to believe that I had dragged myself over every centimetre, every stone, of it.

A cool breeze swept across the plateau. I had been protected from it while in the hollow, but now had to begin moving again before it chilled me. I remembered this stretch to the summit's highest point (known as the trig point). Made up of huge boulders of dolerite that had been split and broken with the repeated freezing and thawing over thousands of years, it was tricky even on two legs. Huge cracks lay in between, some dropping into darkness that gave no indication of their depth. I imagined many a camera being dropped down into them, never to be seen again.

In some ways, *crossing* this sort of terrain was more difficult than actually *climbing*. In climbing, I felt that I actually achieved something with each pull upwards. Moving up and down through these huge cracks seemed to go on forever, seemed to drag out the inevitable. Almost as though the mountain was saying 'Uh-uh. You're not there yet.' I could see the marker most of the time, spurring me on, although it disappeared from view each time I had to drop into the next crack before continuing.

Guided constantly by Brian and Cate; I moved closer and closer.

'This way, Wazza. It looks pretty dodgy over there mate.' They too had become accustomed to my capabilities and were beginning to appreciate that some things that might seem easy for me were actually very difficult.

A crowd had gathered around the trig point now as I approached it: the news crew, Jeremy and Meagan, Cate and Brian. I fought to keep the lump in my throat down, tears threatening to well in my eyes behind my sunglasses. So many emotions threatened to overwhelm me: sheer joy at having achieved something that, only six months before, had seemed gone from my reach forever; the ability just to be out in nature, away from the picnic tables and car parks of the pseudo naturalist; deep sadness at the reality of what had happened to me, what I was now. That this was it, this was how hard it would be for me now to get to the simplest of places; the sort of hiking that I'd surpassed years ago, moving on to more challenging and physically demanding adventures. At the same time I was forced to look at why I put myself into the wilderness at all, especially now, like this.

Was it to feel that achievement, that conquering of a mountain or an inhospitable place? To come out and say, 'It might have been tough, but I got through it OK'? That physical and mental challenge. Or was it because of the enormous peace I felt when surrounded by nature, the all-encompassing feeling of being part of the world, being able to stand back and see your place in it? Giving us an opportunity to get a glimpse into our very soul. Pushing the questions from my mind, I took a deep breath and moved forward . . .

Shuffling the last few metres just as carefully as I had every step of the way . . . reaching out and grabbing the frame of the summit marker, I climbed underneath it. To the encouragement of everybody there, I could almost *feel* their support for me, their willing me on, in the air. Moving to the centre of the frame, I sat with the trig plate between what remained of my legs, and placed a hand on it.

'That'll do me.'

EPILOGUE

For the record, Geert van Keulen *did* have a permit to climb Mount Bowen, along with a route description issued to him in Townsville. Although I didn't have a permit myself, I justified my right to climb with Geert because simple bushwalking ethics warn against travelling alone.

I have accepted that what happened to me was simply an act of nature, and that sometimes 'shit just happens'.

Warren Macdonald
January 1999